God Why Me?

I0541708

How I Survived Life's Trials With Grace, Music and Life-Changing Affirmations

S. TOMEASE JONES

Disclaimer:

All names have been changed to protect the innocent and guilty parties involved. Some references have been altered to not incriminate myself or others.

DEDICATION

To those who have felt the world's weight was on their shoulders, when life seemed to be better without you in it...

Well, I'm here to tell you

You Are Loved, You Are Worthy, and You are NEEDED.

Allow yourself some grace in knowing that dreams are never denied, just delayed.

The darkness of night never lasts too long before the light of day shines through.

It was all necessary for your growth.

Trust me, the journey gets better.

This one's for you.

CONTENTS

ACKNOWLEDGMENTS

I give all thanks, honor, and praise to God for allowing me to use the gift that He has given me. Even when I thought I wouldn't be great, you already knew I was. Thank you, Daddy! I don't take it for granted.

To my 4 amazing children, you are each a gift from the heavens. I'm so honored to have been chosen to give you life. You motivate me to be a better mother and advocate for you and others. Each of you has aided in my freedom and liberation. Without you all, I would not have made it, seriously. Having you all kept me pushing and kept me striving. From the depths of my soul, I thank you. We're in this together, always, love Mom.

To my mother, Cheryl. God rest your soul. Thank you for helping me realize my true potential of all that I could be, despite all that I endured. I know you gave me the best of you, even when you didn't realize that for yourself. You made me a better version of you, and I'm so glad to carry out all that you wanted to do and more for your family. You were my Mom, my teacher of the streets, and my very best friend. Physically you're gone, but spiritually you've NEVER left me. Even in transition, you are here, still guiding and protecting me. I am forever grateful for your undying love.

To my father, LB… I'm so thankful for you being in my life. For many years I carried resentment towards you for not being around in my formative years. What I realized is that God protected me from what life could have been had you been there. I realize that during those times, you weren't in the right headspace to be the father I needed. I just want to say that even in your absence, I learned everything I needed to be able to love myself effectively. You've become a vital part of my life, and I love and respect you for everything you've done to change your life and mine. Love you, Dad.

Special shout-outs to my siblings… Thank you for being my 1st set of kids. You all have been the catalyst in forming my journey as a parent, good and bad alike. I appreciate and love you all. Just know that any success I have is a win for us all.

To Baby Joe, thank you for being the safety net I needed when I felt I didn't have one. You are no longer here, but I still feel you pushing me in the background every time I fall. Or I'll see something that reminds me of you, and I laugh. You were more of a father to me than your OWN child. I'm sorry you never got a chance to really connect with your son, but I'm forever grateful for all that you added to my life. The memories will stay with me forever. As long as I talk about our memories, you're never REALLY gone at all. Your spirit hears, listens, and feels the love. I miss you so much, and I will always be your "Baby Love."

To Aunt Janet, I thank you for being my first teacher. You instilled that love of reading, writing, and creativity early. I remember how you would have me act out a song as if I were performing on stage. Omg, I was such a goofy kid. I love that you helped me to tap into just being free in who I was and who I wanted to be. We don't talk as much anymore, but you will always be loved for the roles you played in my life. The good times made me happy, and the worst times made me strong… Thank you.

To Granny, you are the matriarch of our family. You've been the constant in ALL our lives. I know that you've had a hard life, and many times you weren't appreciated or acknowledged for all the good you did. I remember the stories you've told me about your upbringing, and when I reminisce, it hurts my heart. Everybody wants to be genuinely loved, and I'm sorry that you didn't always get that. Those voids helped form some of the hardened emotions you've carried for so long. We weren't always on the best terms, but I would not have made it without you. You've pushed me at times to be uncomfortable in my own space. Looking back, I wouldn't change a thing; because it allowed me to change for the better. Always know that you are appreciated, loved, and honored every day I'm alive. I'm an extension of you and will forever make you proud, whether you acknowledge it or not. I love you Helen.

To all my other family not mentioned, EACH of you has helped to shape and mold me in ways you may not ever understand. I've been able to gain strength, wisdom, and knowledge from you all. I give thanks to you for pouring into me.

To Shamecca, girl, " You So Crazy," This is our inside joke. You were the first to show me how to embrace all the bad and use it to push myself further by example. You were just another girl like me that had been through hell and back and just wanted to make it out of the chaos. I've admired you, your tenacity, drive, and faith used to get you through. I'm so glad to have met you, and I know Mama Cheeks is beaming with pride every day. I miss her and your Dad; he was hilarious. VSU and our experience will ALWAYS be near and dear to my heart. We don't talk as often as we used to but know that you will always be my sister. Love you.

To my Girl, Mary, it's been roughly 20 years. We go way back. Thank you, Sis, for your endless support, photoshoots, and "Artzy Girl" swag. You've pushed me in ways that I never thought possible while loving me through it all. Love you, Girl.

To my Girl, Vee, much gratitude to you for being a different voice of reason when I've felt like I've gone too far. You inspire me and push me to be excellent in my later stage of life. I pray that you get your story out next because the WORLD needs to hear it.

To my Spiritual Coach Jessica, a MILLION thank you's for showing me the tools I already had to operate in my higher self. You are the BOMB.COM. Thank you for your constant support, reassurance, love, kindness, and friendship along this road we call life. You were sent for this period of my life, and I'm so grateful for the guiding light you bring.

A special thank you goes out to my Clubhouse family members. Dominique, Luv & Victoria, thank you for being an instrumental part of my growth and progression. I appreciate you all. Your friendship goes far beyond social media. To Robin Young, Sarah Ausby, Ardenay Gardner, and Apostle Deborah Anderson, thanks to EACH of you for exemplifying what female leadership looks like. Thank you for pushing my limits creatively, professionally, personally, AND spiritually. I've officially been "*un-muted*"! I'm so grateful to be a part of your sisterhood. God knew exactly what I needed when He allowed us to cross paths.

I would be remiss without giving thanks to the one man in my life who can seem like a thorn at times, yet STILL loves me to the finish line. David, you have become more than a cohort, a prayer buddy, and business partner to me. You have become my confidant, ride or die, and very best friend. You are the iron that sharpens my iron. You've shown me genuine love past my pain, and for that I honor you. Thank you for allowing me to share my goals and dreams with you, with no judgment, and for riding the waves with me. Thank you for diving into my misery and bringing me to shore. I love you to life Crouch. Here's to a couple of forevers.

I **have** to shout out to my angel in the outfield, Sonja Graves. Thank you for editing at the last minute. God always has a "ram in the bush." Thank you for being my friend in a time of need. I'm forever grateful.

Extra, EXTRA special thanks to Corey Cross and the entire Webs of Color Design Team. Thank you for believing and supporting my vision, while executing it with excellence and superiority. You've helped me to create a brand that speaks my name before I walk in the room. What you do, and what you've done is nothing short of AMAZING! Here's to many more business opportunities, books, and years of friendship as well.

I could name so many others, near and far, but I don't have the time or space. So many people have impacted my life over the years. Just know that YOU WERE NEEDED. And I wouldn't be here at this appointed time without you.

And lastly, to the past men in my life, whether we were talking, had a friendship, in a relationship, or even a "situationship". I thank you most of all. During those times, I discovered what is truly important and what I DON'T want in my life. I didn't value myself, didn't love myself, and I looked to you to validate me. But I'm so grateful that the light bulb came on, and now I'm a better version of myself, and I owe that to you all. All the "love bombing" and "gas-lighting" made me learn to love myself without you. The accusations taught me to trust myself more and not waver in my truth. I learned the meaning of "trauma bonding" from each of my relationships and how a half truly doesn't make a whole. You have to be whole in order to be HEALED. I knew my healing would emanate eventually, and I'm so thankful that God allowed me to embrace it. We all connected through a place of pain, and I'm just glad that now I no longer wallow in mine.

And the TRUTH shall set me free.

PREFACE

I wrote a poem called the "Lotus Flower" over ten years ago, and I know it was divinely ordained. It talked about how we are like seeds being planted, brought into this world with *gifts* and intentions of added *beauty* and *substance*. Yet many of us experience different elements that can hinder us from achieving our mission. Those that stay the course throughout it all will be the ones to discover that their **failures**, **pitfalls**, and **mishaps** were NEEDED for their transformation.

I've gone from one crisis to another in my life. Often these moments of life were beyond my control and forced upon me through my upbringing. At which other times, my self-doubt and limiting beliefs kept me from making conscious decisions that inevitably impeded my *growth and stability*. For a long time, while a part of organized religion, I valued a lot of the messages of *empowerment* I heard over the years. I found that even during those times, life seemed well externally, but internally I was still the same. The **anxiety**, **worry**, **self-doubt**, and **self-sabotaging** thoughts had become second nature, and I didn't know how to function without them.

It's been in my heart to write a book for years now. I believe this time is the proper alignment for this gift to be delivered. I used to think to myself, "Who wants to hear my story?" "Will it even make a difference?" And it took me back to when I was pregnant with my son. My children and I were in a homeless shelter where I lived after his birth. I remember feeling lost and confused when he was around a year and a half. I was going to church, but it felt like nothing was changing. I had a job but still couldn't maintain stability for my family. I felt **defeated, lonely**, and **ridiculed** for not being the *good mother* everyone thought I should be.

Each night before putting the kids to bed, I would play a song to put them to sleep. It was called "Chasing After You" by Tye Tribbett & God's Authority. And as the words resonated in my spirit, I burst into tears. I whimpered, not wanting to wake up the kids. With tears streaming down my face, I said, "God, WHY ME? Why must I be the one to endure ALL the time? Nobody else in my family has it as rough as I do. It seems like I'm ALWAYS going through something." And it was at that moment I heard the spirit of God respond to me with the rhetorical question, "Why NOT you, Shawaun?" I thought to myself, "Am I dreaming?" But then I heard the still, small voice again, "Why not you? I allowed you to go through these things because I knew you could withstand the weight. Your sisters wouldn't survive it, and your friends can't do it, ONLY you. I have a purpose that I need YOU to fulfill. Just know these situations I'm allowing are not because you did anything wrong. Its so others can see my spirit within you. Your story will bring me *Glory*." And with that, my journey of *self-discovery* began, little did I know. At that moment, I no longer blamed God for my struggles. From this day forward, I knew that my journey was for people to watch me move through my trials with grace.

This book represents my discovery of who I was all along. Trials and tribulations are presented to just about everyone at some period of our lives. It's about knowing how to maneuver during those times that determine how well you finish. Thankfully, I'm at a place of acceptance in my life where I can perceive those moments as God telling me to *look within*. Lessons and messages can be given, but like seeds, if you aren't appropriately watered, you won't grow. And if you aren't growing, you're dying. Looking to be watered by others may not happen. You must find ways to replenish and encourage yourself. I'm still learning this day by day.

I was raised by the golden rule and believed that people would treat me as I treated them. Boy, have I been mistaken. Yet, it doesn't change the genetic makeup of who I am. I've been burned by many, but the fire hasn't scarred me.

Being an *empath* has afforded me to connect with people on an emotional and spiritual level. I instinctively feel their pain and want to offer compassion and peace. This is an example of human nature, but we must have a threshold on how far we extend ourselves to others.

People-pleasing can disrupt the intended direction of your life. It can cause you to divert the path made for you because you're so busy trying to appease someone else on their journey. It can be **draining** physically, mentally, and spiritually. We each have our own paths to be held accountable for here in the physical realm. When we truly tap into the inner reasons for our existence and the power that we have within us, this is how we gain the clarity needed to live the life of our dreams. No more **worry** or **overwhelming** thoughts to keep us up late at night. I consider this book a tool in my own personal *healing*. Each word I've written brings up memories where I burst into *laughter* or flood with tears. In this, all I can say is thank you, because I survived it all. This is a first-hand look at my life from my perspective, displaying the good, bad, and ugly. Showing that even with all the damaging scars from the continuous pressure, I've been cut like a beautiful diamond. I heard a friend of mine once say, "Confession is good for the soul but bad for the reputation," which I find to be true more now that I'm making myself vulnerable to public scrutiny.

Let me tell you a quick story. I touch on it a bit later in this book, but I want to show you how we hold onto stories that aren't true. When I was a young child, I developed seemingly overnight. I wasn't thinking about sex, although many girls my age were already active. I had a situation where a doctor misdiagnosed me with an **STD**, and although it was later confirmed incorrect, I was **never given an apology**. My grandmother basically made me **feel like shit**. Like I was a filthy rag that someone had mutilated from constant use. I was still a virgin and didn't give up my virginity until I was 19 years old. But here I was, being accused of having a disease that I couldn't possibly have contracted. And a situation happened recently that triggered me so deeply that it caused me to burst into tears.

I went to visit my family back in my hometown and stayed with my grandmother. Things went well, and the visit was nice, but weeks later, it was as if she had a bit of an attitude toward me when I called. I wasn't quite sure what it could be, so I didn't address it. We normally talk at least two to three times a week, and she usually calls me first. But for two weeks, I heard nothing from her. I called to see how she was doing, and I got the coldest response from her. "Hi," she said in a matter-of-fact manner. I continued with the conversation but could tell that she really didn't have much interest in speaking to me. I got off the phone feeling puzzled and a bit confused. Almost as if I was being left in the dark about something that I was not aware of. I called my daughter only to discover that I had been the topic of conversation for weeks about something I supposedly did. I immediately called back my grandmother to ask what the issue was, as if I knew nothing of it at first.

"Granny, what's going on? Did I do something to you that I'm not aware of?"

"Well, if you DID something, then you know what you did," she responded.

"I don't KNOW what I did. That's why I'm asking," I said. She accused me of stealing from her home, and at that moment, it took me back. I felt like that same little girl being accused of something I had no control over.

"What do you mean I stole from you? I've NEVER taken anything from you. This really hurts my feelings. Why would you think I would do anything like this to you?"

"Well, I don't know, I can't pinpoint it. We'll talk about this later." And that was it. Come to find out, this "discussion" had been going on for weeks amongst my family members, and instead of her saying anything to me, she saw fit to tell anyone who would listen to these lies…

What I learned at that moment was how **unhealed** I was. I've been on this journey to rediscover who I am and who I was created to be, only to feel as if I uncovered more pain that was hidden deep within. One thing you have to understand, the process of healing may not always be pretty or comfortable. There may be situations that will spark a memory that you totally forgot, and you now have to face it. I really had to sit with this, even though I wanted to dismiss it altogether.

What I realized is that I had given my Granny **too much power**. She is the one person I had allowed to **dictate** and **puppeteer** my entire life. When you give someone authority to reign over you, you no longer have any sense of control, thus finding yourself living up to someone else's expectations of you. I thought about all the stories I replayed from my past and how those stories made me believe that I wasn't strong enough, smart enough, or even bold enough to pursue my dreams. As I began to really take the time to evaluate, I was all of those things. Life has afforded me to live through countless situations where I've had to be *brave*, *bold*, *smart* and *strategic* in my moves to best survive.

So many people are living the lies they were told as children and not knowing how to break free from them. What lies have you been told and constantly replaying? What have you been made to believe about yourself? Somewhere in your life, someone has made a comment or accusation that unconsciously shifted doubt into your mindset to keep you from fulfilling your God-given destiny. Well, let me tell you, it's never too late to *reclaim your rightful place*. Those old labels no longer apply in your life. Negative energy and hurtful words can be used to permeate our souls and stagnate us from moving forward if we allow it. I wrote this to prove to myself that I've always been greater than whatever has been said about me. I just needed to remove the rose-colored glasses of pain to believe it for myself.

When you find yourself at the end of this book, please don't pity me. Pity is a low vibrational emotion that does nothing to expand one's growth. Journey with me as I uncover the layers of abandonment, rejection, pain and unforgiveness, to a place of healing and wholeness. I'm learning that the key to life is to find the beauty around you, even in the darkest of times. I hope this book becomes a tool in your healing journey by using my life as an example. Just remember that love is optional, but grace is free. Find freedom in loving who you are, just as you are!

"Then the Lord answered me, and said: Write the vision, and make it plain upon tables, that he may run that readeth it."
- Habakkuk 2:2 (NKJV)

CHAPTER 1

FLY LIKE AN EAGLE

The process from conception to birth is amazing. To know that a microscopic egg is fertilized by one of the millions of sperm cells aiming at it. The intricate way cells intertwine systematically to create a human being is mind-blowing. Our bodies begin to form while our minds shape how we will think, interpret, listen, and ingest everything around us. I believe that somewhere in the process of conception, that's when our spirits determine who and where we will be brought forth from. We ultimately "choose" our paths in the spirit realm to carry out the intended purpose through whatever vessel we select. God has a natural way of ensuring that we emerge from the same vessel necessary for our destiny. Even down to the names we were given, it adds up to a much more important purpose. My mother, Cheryl, had no clue that I was destined to fly like an eagle in this world. But she believed I would be someone great.

I was born during the bicentennial year on June 6, in Richmond, Virginia. The world was in full disco swing, and it was the beginning of the summer heat. Here you have a 21-year-old girl, just becoming an adult, out partying, hanging with friends, and now a mother to a baby girl. I can only imagine how my mom felt. From excitement and joy to fear and worry, she was unsure if she would be a good mom. But like all parents, you don't think about the worst or try not to, at least. You just continue to think positively about the journey you and this little one has ahead of you.

I see that my mother and I were genuinely connected from the first day we laid eyes on each other. It would be a bond that would surpass life and even death. Our spirits are like one, and I believe we channeled each other's energy on more than one occasion over the years. She was always there, even when she wasn't physically. She was in my thoughts, dreams, shoot, even some of my nightmares. It was like she never left my side.

Growing up with my Mom was like a psychedelic road trip sometimes. We grew and discovered life together when we weren't going back and forth between Virginia and Massachusetts. We had some great times. Life was different in the '80s, let me tell you. Kids could roam and do stuff that I wouldn't DARE have my kids do at that age. I was around 4 and 5 years old, going to the store by myself and riding the subway. It was crazy then. People looked out for people, especially kids, so I never felt threatened while going about my way. I remember how my Mom used to give me an allowance every week just because. The only place I wanted to spend it was at the ice cream parlor or the record shop, and they were both on Mass Ave. that was opposite our apartment.

I LOVED listening to music and still do. When Michael Jackson's "Thriller" album came out, my Mom and I were in a heated debate about the title of one of the songs on the album. She said, "Shawaun, that's not it. The song is called Billie Jean." So here I am, 6 years old, thinking I knew EVERYTHING about music. I said boldly, "Uh uh, it's called I Am The One". So, my Mom wanted to prove that she was right, so we walked to the record store, which was roughly ten city blocks away from our house. Lo and behold, she was right. It was indeed "Billie Jean".

I looked a bit disappointed when the store clerk told us the correct title, and she looked at me and said, "It's ok, your title was better anyway." We both laughed walking away singing "Billie Jean" all the way back to the house. In the second grade at King School in Cambridge, my teacher would have dance parties in our classroom every Friday. She allowed us to bring music from home to play while we danced all around the room.

Because I already had such an extensive record collection, it was no wonder that I was designated the class DJ every week to bring in the music. That morning, my Mom decided she would bring the music to my school so I wouldn't be late. I was usually late just about every day. My Mom would always say, "Well, better late than never". My Mom planned a huge surprise for me that day. She had gone to the record store and bought the full Michael Jackson album that had just been released that week. When she walked into my class and showed everyone the cover, ALL the kids were like, "OOOH, Shawaun! You got the Michael Jackson album! I WISH my Mom was cool like yours." Then everybody started running towards the album cover to look at it. The cover was different from anything we had ever seen at that time. It was like a full cover photo that opened like a book. To see Mike lying on his side with a white tiger…that was the coolest thing ever. Man, I loved my Mom so much that day. She was my best friend and always knew how to make me smile.

Later on, I noticed that my Mom had changed a lot. She was staying out late and not coming home until the wee hours or had more company coming in and out of the house. As a kid, I didn't pay attention at first since I was always in my little fantasy world. I would pretend to be grown out on a date with Prince or one of the boys from New Edition.

I could always tell when something bad was happening because my Mom would come home drunk and stumbling throughout the house.

For a while my Aunt Janice lived with us. My Aunt had moved there first, then my Mom and I left VA and moved in with her. My Aunt had noticed the decline with my Mom long before it worsened, so she moved out, and we occupied the place by ourselves. For a while, it was great because now I had time with my Mom, and I could visit my Aunt at her new place too. I didn't bargain for the day my world would fall apart.

My Aunt was coming to pick me up from the house. I recall a few other people sitting around drunk or high as a kite at our home. My Mom was in her room with the door closed. When my Aunt came in, you could see the look of disgust on her face. Almost as if she just couldn't take any more. For her, things had gone way past her breaking point. She said, "Shawaun, do you want to see what your mother does to herself?" She then proceeded to open the bedroom door where my Mom was. I saw the tourniquet wrapped around her arm while injecting herself with a needle. She said, "See, this is what your mother does." "CLOSE THE DOOR JANICE." my Mom shouted. And with that, I was whisked out of the house. Walking with my Aunt toward the train station all I could think was "why was my Mom doing that?"

In light of my Mom's extracurricular activities, it was close to the summertime, and I LOVED the summers, because I was going to be with my two most favorite people in the whole wide world outside of my Mom and Aunt. That was my Granny and my Uncle Joe in Richmond. Every summer, my Granddaddy would drive 16 hours from Virginia to Massachusetts to pick me up for the entire summer.

I LOVED visiting my Granny and Uncle, who we affectionately called "Baby Joe." He was like a father figure that I didn't have growing up. I remember Baby Joe was a part of a bike club, where he and a group of his friends would meet up at the park down the street from the house and hang out.

They would ride to the numerous free concerts in the neighborhood parks, and guess who rode shotgun? You guessed it, me. I was so small then, so my Uncle would get a hand towel and fold it over the bar of his 12-speed bike, which would be my front-row seat. I would ride in the breeze to all the destinations around town and sometimes had a better view than the other kids at these venues.

I was my Granny's first grandchild, so she spoiled me rotten. I felt so loved being around her. She would take me shopping with her, or sometimes, I would just sit in the kitchen and watch her cook. That was one of my favorite pastimes because she always let me sample whatever she was cooking, and it was always so good. I would cook when my oldest daughter was small, just like my Granny. She always threw get-togethers or parties in our basement, entertaining family and friends. Or she would cook a shit load of food for us to enjoy just because. I believe my Granny loved to see people smiling and enjoying her food. It made her feel even more special whenever people raved over her fried chicken and potato salad. And don't forget about the homemade sweet potato pies. Mmm, those were made special every holiday. They were her signature dishes. She had orders for those multiple times during the year. Or if someone would pass away, my Granny always volunteered to bring a huge Tupperware bowl of fried chicken and potato salad to the repass. I guess that's why I enjoy cooking when I do. I experienced that same feeling my Granny did. That sense of joy and feeling needed by someone. Knowing you are genuinely loved and appreciated by those around you.

It's funny how we can find ourselves mimicking and even replicating experiences in our childhood. It's as if our endorphins expound when recreating those moments that brought us joy or positive memories. Our minds revert to when we felt loved, safe, or secure. You can even remember the smell of foods you loved.

I remember my Granny had a huge backyard that became her garden sanctuary. She enjoyed being out in the dirt, planting flowers or fruit. She had a huge grapevine, blackberries and strawberries growing under the porch, and flowers everywhere. There were so many colors. It was beautiful and peaceful. As a kid, I would go on the back porch steps before sunrise and marvel at how the light from the sun would make the dew sparkle on the grass. For me, it was such a tranquil view. As an escape almost from the way my life was back home. Being in Virginia every summer was like my little piece of heaven. It was just for me, and I loved it.

In 1982, a movie came out called "Annie" about an orphaned girl adopted by a millionaire. Well, I guess I had talked about it so much that Granny decided to surprise me and take me to the movies to see it. We went all the way across town to Cloverleaf mall. In my hometown, Cloverleaf mall was the place to be. I was so excited, walking around and looking at all of the bright lights and busyness going on inside. I could tell Granny was somewhat uncomfortable being there, but looking at the joy on my face was the reassurance she needed to get through the day. The movie was great. I came out singing the melodies throughout the movie. Granny gave me an even BIGGER surprise and took me to the toy store afterward. I bought the figurines from the movie so I could play the movie at home. This was such a great day for me. One that I cherish the most with my Granny. It would be almost 25 years before she and I would go to the movies again. Yet this day would be ingrained in my heart forever.

The connections we form in those pivotal years of development stick with us as we grow older. They form a template of how you are to act, conduct yourself, and be perceived by others around you. My Granny would always say, "You can't go out looking like that. What would people think of me letting you look all sloppy?" It seems harmless, but those critiques became a part of my makeup.

The emotions attached somehow became my own, and I wore them every day. The fear of what "other" people thought fueled how my grandmother operated around others. She presumed that if you maintained the facade of "having it all together," you were good. Having a specific appearance was a focal point for my Granny, from the jewelry she wore to her outfits. When it was a special occasion or a funeral, that was her time to shine. She was always well-dressed and with food in hand, ready to serve the people at the event. One thing I will say is that my Granny was always serving people. Whether it was with her food, time, cleaning people's houses, or helping out those in need.

My Granny was a country girl. She was raised in New Kent and was one of 13 children born to her parents. She was born on her mother's birthday, March 8, and always flowing in her Piscean energy. Granny told me lots of stories about her life as a child. Like how she and her brothers would go out in the field and eat red clay, or how her Dad would kill the chickens by swinging their necks, then throwing them down on the log to cut their heads off for skinning. Gruesome imagery, I know, but that was her life. Very simplistic. At times she said they didn't have much, so her Mom would make biscuits, and each child would get one, or a piece of one, and sop it in some fatback grease, and THAT was breakfast. Sometimes she said she wouldn't get anything. She said her father was somewhat mean to her because she was the darkest in complexion of all the girls. He ostracized her in many ways. Back then, it wasn't an uncommon issue. In the Black community, we still struggle with skin color complexity.

To me, my Granny had the most beautiful skin. I would always tell her how soft her skin was. Her cheeks were so supple and blemish-free. She's still beautiful to me at the ripe age of 95 years, she's still alive and kicking. When she was 18 and graduating high school, her mother bought her a watch from the Montgomery Ward catalog. Granny said she loved the token of affection from her mother. However, she overheard her father arguing with her mother about the watch that night.

He said, "Why did you buy her that damn watch?" She heard her mother defending her decision, but it hurt her heart to listen to them bicker. She always felt her father didn't care for her, which proved it. So, she packed her bags.

The following day she went to her mother with the watch in hand and said, "I appreciate it, but take it back," and then left for the city, never to return.

As a child, I was very astute and read the newspaper by age 4. My family members have taught me something different to add to my being. Baby Joe introduced me to the love of music very early on. He would play music or sing to put me to sleep. I knew of so many songs from the 60's and 70's, along with the artists' names. We would play "name that tune" all the time. My Aunt introduced me to a love for reading. She would take me to the library and read to me before bed. Sometimes, she would pull out the tape recorder, and we would make our books on tape. One of my favorite books she would read was "Stevie" by John Steptoe. It was by a black author, and the illustrations were riveting to me. It embodied the struggle behind the story, a struggle I knew all too well in my community.

I'm telling you; the mind is a beautiful thing. That was well over 40 years ago, and I still remember it like it was yesterday. I remember the feeling of sitting beside my Aunt and listening to her act out the story. She would use different tones and inflections to bring the story to life. I learned so much from her. For a long time, I wanted to be just like her. She epitomized to me what an educated black woman looked like. She wasn't even a high school graduate, but no one knew or remotely thought otherwise. She was well-versed and articulate and could talk to anyone in any environment. She would "talk white" while conducting business and then talk in slang when around people she knew. She always projected a polished, educated demeanor, one of versatility. I guess she inherited that trait from my Granny of learning how to hide behind a facade.

My Granny and Baby Joe spent most of their days working and would unwind by sitting on the front porch. They would tell gossip stories while sipping on some homemade sun tea which was my uncle Baby Joe's specialty. Sometimes they would be out there for hours, laughing and joking. Back then, you could stay out there and sleep through the night without anyone bothering you. Since I was the only child in the family, I picked up many adult mannerisms early on. The way the adults would talk about stuff was how I did. My family said it got to the point where I spoke too much. I was always running my mouth. There would be times when they would say, "Damn Shawaun, you talk too much." or "Where in the world did you get that from?" I was able to talk about current events as if I knew what was going on. I had confidence then that allowed me to feel free and uninhibited by the world around me. I thought I was safe around them, despite them slowly putting me in a box. When stones are thrown at you, the first ones that hit hurt because they catch you off guard. Over time, the more that's thrown, the less likely you feel the sting and the number you become. Don't get me wrong; it still hurts like hell. It just affects you differently and begins to penetrate you internally.

My body was embarking on the learned lessons of pain and how to adapt to it," take a licking and keep on ticking," like a Timex watch. The highs and lows of my childhood would not only cultivate my existence but create the imagery of how my life would play out and the capacity to learn from it. So far, I've shown you how the mind and body correlate together. How cognitively, we carry emotions attached to us as they become embedded in our consciousness. Our spirits are designed to capture our core beliefs and tie them to every area of our lives. The spirits within my family took significant precedence in my progression. These were my first teachers in life. And while they were all learning as they went along, I know they wanted to instill the very "best" of themselves into me. Unfortunately, I got a taste of the worst too.

After that incident of watching my Mom shoot up, she was so ashamed; we didn't spend as much time together anymore. She would have my Aunt pick me up more often. Or I would stay with my favorite great Aunt, Martha, who was my father's Aunt, after school. She was the twin sister of my Dad's Mom. She lived right across the street in Putnam Gardens Public Housing. She was my only real connection to my father's side of the family. He didn't claim me, nor did his mother. When he would see me, it was as if I didn't exist; or at least that's how I felt. It's funny how the mind will make you believe things that may or may not be true. You take in the emotion and hold on to it for dear life, as it becomes your logic at that moment.

I couldn't fathom why my Dad treated me so cold, and I thought he didn't care. In reality, he was battling his own demons with drugs and alcohol, so half the time, he was too out of it anyway to even recognize who I was. At home, the roles had now switched. I was no longer the daughter; I had officially taken over as the parent. I found myself responsible for ensuring my Mom stayed "on point." I had to protect my Mom at all costs from the bad men in and out of her bed, the late nights out, and even the fights she would get into from being drunk. I had to learn to become her voice of reason when at times, she had none.

My Mom was what some would call a street thug. She was a genuine gangsta. Growing up, she was like a bully and was always getting in trouble at school for fighting. Granny would say that my Mom was so mean and was always at school regarding her behavior. As she got older, it progressed, and she fought men and women alike, she didn't care. As a little girl, it seemed as if she had no fear.

Contrary to belief, she had a gentle side that many didn't get the opportunity to see. She loved to laugh and was a jokester and quick-witted. Her moments of unmotherly behavior made me realize how afraid and fearful she was. Her life was out of control, and she didn't know how to get a hold of it.

As an adult, I now understand why my Mom resorted to drugs, alcohol, and prostitution as a means of escape. She was escaping the pain of her childhood, her life choices, and her failures. Some people can't bounce back and recover when they fumble. My Mom was one of many during the era when drugs changed the dynamics of the family. I became a latchkey kid after that fateful day. My Mom was either gone "to work" or passed out from a drug high. It's funny, though, that with all that I knew of my Mom, I never looked at her with any less love; if anything, I loved her more. The next thing I knew, my Mom had calmed down a bit and wasn't going out as much, nor was she drinking heavily. I noticed she had a guy around all the time. He would come to the house, or we would meet him somewhere, and he would walk and talk with her. To me, he was old. Way too old to be with my Mom. I'd often see him wearing a postal uniform, so I figured he was a mailman or something.

My Aunt would tease my Mom about it, calling the man her "Sugar Daddy". Then I would go around singing the song by Jean Wright called "Mr. Big Stuff." She would follow behind her, singing, "Mr. Big Stuff . Who do you think you are? Mr. Big Stuff, you're never going to get my love." Then one day, my Mom came to me and said, "You're gonna be a big sister." Oh my gosh. I was super excited. I would have a baby to teach everything I learned in school. When my Mom found out she was having a girl, I felt like God had answered my prayers. I couldn't wait to have her around, and I counted the days. I watched my Mom's belly grow with this life inside her. I would rub her belly in anticipation of the beautiful little person I was going to meet. The day my Mom went into labor, it was early in the morning. We didn't have a house phone, so we had to walk up this steep hill to get from our apartment on Green St. to the YMCA up on Mass. Ave. I went back to visit for the summer years later and went by that street. It seemed a lot less intimidating as a young adult than when I was 7. My Mom was calling the ambulance to meet us there, as her contractions became more robust with each step. The ambulance came, and we both got in the back.

We were on our way to Brigham & Women's Hospital in Boston. It was close to 7 a.m., and my Mom kept saying, "I can't hold it," trying to hold back the urge to push. As soon as we were right around the corner from the hospital, my Mom couldn't hold it anymore and gave one last push. My sister was born. I believe it was 6:59 a.m. on September 6, 1984. I was right there to see it all. All in my Mom's coochie, watching the miracle of life, front row and center. Man, what an experience! To watch this person, grow inside my Mom's belly, and now she is here. She was so beautiful to me. She was like a little doll baby I could play with. I couldn't wait to get her back home. During my Mom's stay in the hospital, I was with my Aunt until her release, thinking of how time was slippin into my new future.

CHAPTER 2

I'VE GOT A NEW ATTITUDE

So much was changing in my young life, yet many things remained the same. Now that my sister was born, things were getting worse at home. My Mom would be out all night sometimes and would come home in the morning when I was ready for school. My Mom was out, and my sister didn't have any formula. I had to improvise and make her a bottle of sugar water so she would go to sleep. I was sitting on the sofa, scared and alone. While sitting there, I looked into my Mom's room and saw a woman's head sitting on top of the shelf in the closet. It was a very dark-skinned woman, and it was as if she was staring right at me. I was super scared, but this wouldn't be the first time that I would see spirits. My Mom's situation worsened, so my Granny decided to have my baby sister, and I come to live with her. She and my grandfather drove up to Massachusetts, packed all our things, and moved us to Virginia. I was coming up on my 9th birthday in a few months by this time. I now had to start over in a new school.

It wasn't like my old school at all. The kids were superficial, unlike what I was used to at home. One little girl came over and teased me every day, saying my hair was too short. The funny thing about it was her hair was shorter than mine. Go figure. It was a bit of an adjustment being in a whole new environment and adapting, but I was resilient.

The main thing that I loved the most was that I could finally be with my two favorite people all the time. I would always hang out with my neighbor down the street.

Angenette was like a big sister to me, and her parents were nice too. Her mother was one of the teachers at the elementary school that I was attending.

I would ride to school with her every day and do my homework at her house after school. She was such a sweetheart. I genuinely miss Mrs. Rivers. She made such an impact in my life; little did she know. She became the peace I needed.

Angenette's parents were both educators. Mrs. Rivers was a member of Delta Sigma Theta sorority, and Mr. Rivers was a member of the Omega Psi Phi fraternity. They had emblems all over their home representing their respective organizations. I'd never seen so much purple and gold or the color red and elephants as I did in their home, the elephants are the symbol for the Deltas. It was like they both created a shrine. They stressed the importance of education and going to college. Angenette was a teenager in high school and looked at me as her little sister. Every summer, I was at their house, and now that I live here permanently, their house had become my solstice. I was always asked to tag along when she had events going on.

I remember they had a family reunion and wanted me to come. They had family coming from the Tidewater area and other various locations. We stayed at this hotel located on The Boulevard in that was like my first time staying in a hotel. It was so cool. I felt a bit uncomfortable, being that these weren't my family members. I found myself adopting what I had learned about "putting on the facade" not to draw much attention. All these people were college-educated or successful in their own right, unlike my family. I didn't have any images of this in my family. I had drugs, liquor, jail, and housekeeping. That was it. Not to throw shade on my family, but I felt entirely out of place and carried out the performance as best I could.

While in the hotel, a concert was happening that weekend at the Coliseum. The Whispers and Teena Marie were performing there.

I would listen to both of their songs with Baby Joe in the basement, and he favored The Whispers as well. To my surprise, as we were leaving the hotel at the end of the weekend, we were walking out, and a big motorcoach bus was parked out front. When I turned around, I saw The Whispers coming out towards the bus. I was star-struck, but I managed to get their autographs before getting on the bus. There wasn't a huge need for security for performing artists back then. Back then, they had more freedom and the ability to be friendly and engaging with their fans.

That Christmas was when the Cabbage Patch Doll came out. There was mass hysteria all over the country of people trying to buy one for their kids. It even became brutal in some areas. The news depicted people standing in lines for hours and even crushing others as they ravaged the aisles and shelves. These dolls became a world phenomenon. Luckily, my Granny was able to get me one. I remember she was brown-skinned like me, with brown yarn hair with pony-tailed braids on each side. She had a blue dress with white ruffled trim around the sleeves and bottom. And it was a red bow right under the neck. I took that doll everywhere. Now I did have another doll at the time, which was my all-time favorite. It was a Holly Hobby doll that I named "Molly." I had her for as long as I could remember. My earliest memory of Molly was when I was around three, maybe. I even took her with me to college when I got older. Molly was with me for years before falling apart and disintegrating when I had to discard her. She was my road dog, for real. I miss you, Molly.

When it was time for Angenette to go to college, I helped her pack her things. She had decided to attend an HBCU, Hampton University in Hampton, VA. As we counted down the days, I was excited for her, but I felt like I was losing my friend. It was beginning to feel like anyone I grew close to would leave me.

Soon it was "Moving day". We all packed up the car and headed to the school. I remember the drive there. I had never been to that area, so the view was amazing. The school campus was huge. It had lush green grass and was amidst a beautiful body of water. This campus was like nothing I had ever seen. It was magical to me. We put her things in her dorm and helped get things together. Watching her made me want to go to college and have my dorm room decorated like hers. If I'm not mistaken, her best friend from high school, Debbie, was her roommate. I remember her coming over to the house a lot. I knew a lot of Angenette's friends, and they all treated me as if I was her little sister in real life.

Over the next few months, things began to sour at Granny's house. This move wasn't what I had imagined it to be at all. She wasn't like the Granny that I remembered from the summer vacations. She was mostly focused on my sister now since she was a baby. It was as if I didn't even exist in her world anymore. When I would try to help her, it was like she grew irritated by me being around her. Or when I would try to hug her, she would pull me off. After my birthday, I began putting on more weight. Up to now, I was very skinny. Granny would have to make extra holes in my belt so that my pants could stay up. She now started calling me names like "fat ass" or "stupid" when she wanted my attention or when I wasn't doing something right. Even when trying to make her happy, she would still find something negative to say.

I'll admit I was a bit of a gossiper at this age. Rightfully so, that was all I saw my family do when I visited. I would go to the neighbors' houses and come home and tell all of their business and vice versa. My Granny hated that I was telling the neighbors what was going on under her roof; she didn't like that shit at all. When it came to people knowing her business or what was happening in the house, she would always say, "What goes on in THIS house, stays in THIS house." And you better not go and talk about it either!

My Granny was a heavy-handed woman who had a mean backhand which I would find out firsthand a few years later. I would think to myself, "Well, it's not a problem when YOU talk about other people and their business. So why is it a problem when I do it?"

Six months passed, and my Mom decided to come and visit my sister and me. I was so excited and missed seeing my Mom on a day-to-day basis. We talked on the phone, but I couldn't talk that much because my Granny didn't make many long-distance calls. Plus, you didn't make calls of your own without asking, especially long-distance ones. I remember how I would sneak and call my Great Aunt Martha. She was more of my grandmother than her twin was, who was my real grandma. I also would call my best friend, Tippany Carenelli. Since kindergarten, she and I had been friends, and we lived on the same block of Green St. until she and her Mom moved to Pleasant St. Oh my God, I remember when Granny started to pay more attention to the growing phone bill. I didn't tell her that I was calling my friend Tippany. I think my Granny had asked my Aunt to investigate and found out the number belonged to a "white woman." Tippany and her Mom are Italian, but they both have naturally blonde hair. My Granny was livid. She accused my Granddaddy of having an affair with this woman. My Granddaddy was something else, but I couldn't let the heated arguments continue and every time he denied it. He was in fact, telling the truth this time. These types of scenes were a recurring norm for me. I eventually came clean about the calls, however. Granny then punished me for a while before giving me my own private phone line in my room to make calls and not tie up her line. I could make long-distance calls, but I had to ask first.

When my family would argue or fight, I would hide under Granny's dining room table. That became my haven or my "base," like in the game of tag. When it stormed really bad, I would get scared and hide under there. It felt like the sky was opening with all of the thunder and lightning.

Granny would always say it was the "Lord doing his work". I would hide and pretend that I was somewhere, ANYWHERE else but where I was. When my Mom came, I was so glad to see her and gave her the biggest hug ever. Each day I wanted to be around my Mom more. In my mind, no one else existed that was more important. I live with my Granny now, so it wasn't like when I would just visit. Now it was my Mom, whom I didn't see often, and I wanted as much time as I could get before she had to leave. I sensed Granny didn't like this ideology too much. I believe she was a bit jealous of it and found ways to deter me from being around my Mom.

I believe my Mom ended up going out with one of our cousins, and of course, had too much to drink. She came in emotional, and everything held back was coming out, ALL at once... She was yelling, crying, and sobbing everywhere. This moment of confession didn't go well, and soon a back-n-forth argument between her and my Granny ensued. Unfortunately, I was front row center, trying to find a way to intervene somehow to stop them both. I heard sirens in the distance, so I knew one of the many neighbors watching had called the police. Damn, here I am, 9 years old, watching the people I love going head-to-head. They began to throw hands, meaning engaging in a fistfight.

In my mind, I'm building up the courage to jump in and defend my Mom. Once again, I felt helpless and out of control. So, I did what I did best, I ran to my room, pulled out my notebook, and started writing. I had already had about three notebooks I used to voice my emotions, fears, dislikes, or random shit I wanted to say. I would call my Aunt and talk with her about stuff I was dealing with and disgruntled about. I would talk about a situation going on, and she would offer her advice on how to handle it. But what was funny to me was that every time I would express my grievances, My Granny would come right back at me, and shit would be worse. I realized that everything I had confided in her, she was going back telling my Granny ALL of it. This was the one person I had grown to trust over everybody. Now I felt betrayed and no longer had that safe space with her.

My Mom ended up going back to Massachusetts because the tension in the household became thick while she was there. Now my Mom is gone. My Granny is mad at me for telling people stuff, and the one I trusted breached my confidentiality. So, the person left to find the solstice was Uncle Baby Joe. Baby Joe was an awesome man to me in his way. He was super creative, and I felt that part of our connection. He was a photographer and loved to take pictures of everyone. He was a singer and could really sing. He was very melodic and taught me everything I know about music. He would sit in the basement for hours, just listening to music most of the time. The funny thing was that each song had a memory attached, so he would take me on his "back down memory lane" journey and reminisce.

Whatever the theme, he had a story in his life attributed to it. One thing about my Uncle, he was a great storyteller. He would sit you down while depicting the scenario, and if you closed your eyes, you would "feel" as if you were right there with him; it was that vivid. You felt like you were in the moment with him. You could see the colors and scenery; he painted the picture with his words. I loved my uncle so much. Unfortunately, my Uncle battled his inner demons and his drug addiction. I would often see him sit in the chair and begin to doze off, literally. It was as if his head was so heavy that he couldn't hold it up. And I would sit there and watch him. I'd think to myself, "Why is he so sleepy? Why is he so exhausted all the time?"

A few months later, I noticed my Uncle hadn't come home. When I answered the phone, the voice said, "You have a collect call from Joe at the Richmond City Jail. Do you accept the call?" I was like, "Granny, it's a collect call from Baby Joe," so I handed my Granny the phone. She talked to him for a while and then said he wanted to speak to me. My Uncle didn't want me to worry and said he was "on vacation" and would be back in a couple of months. Of course, by this time, I was young, but I wasn't stupid for real.

I knew he was "vacationing" in a jail cell. NONE of my family was ever truthful. They wanted to shield me with" little white lies."

At this point, I had seen so much and been exposed to so much that there was nothing that I wasn't aware of. I was a lot smarter than they anticipated, but I never questioned or contested the deception. Over time it just compounded all the damage. It was like they ALL were living a double life, a physical vs. a mental one. Now my sister is getting older and at an age where she's learning her ABC's and 123's, along with shapes and colors. I was like her school teacher, and she was in my class. I felt like my Aunt when she taught me all those things. She would do little things to irritate me because she knew my Granny would defend her every time. I remember my Granny often telling her, "Leave Shawaun alone. You know she is crazy." It's funny how words can shape your perception and your attitude. Time for everybody to get a new one if you ask me. Never knew how many lessons I would have to learn because of it.

CHAPTER 3

WHEN DOVES CRY

The year is 1986, and life was nostalgic for me. I was living in everyone else's fantasy while trying to create my own. My 10th birthday was approaching, and I was super hype about it. At school, things were going okay. It had been about a year or so since starting at Ginter Park Elementary, where I attended. I was adjusting fairly well, I guess. My 4th-grade teacher, Mrs. Ellis, was very strict. The good thing was I made sure I did my work so that she wouldn't turn on me. All over the news, they've been talking about how they are planning another trip to the moon. The school was making sure all the 4th and 5th-grade classes had a TV in the room to watch the live broadcast. I'm kinda excited, but it doesn't interest me too much. All I could think of was how I could get away from my life because, in my mind, it SUCKED. January 28, 1986, started off like any other day. Granny would wake me up around 5 a.m. to do my hair and fix me breakfast before she went to work. At the time, she was working at one of the private universities in the area as a Custodian. I loved it when she let my sister and I go to work with her when the college kids were out; we had so much fun. After she left, I got dressed and went back to bed until it was time for me to meet Mrs. Rivers, two houses down, to get to school.

When walking into my class, everyone was chatty, and they already had the television in the room so we could watch the live launch. I remember it was a beautiful day.

Sun was shining bright, and we were all ready to be a part of a historic moment. My teacher even allowed us to have some orange juice and doughnuts while we were watching. In my mind, this was starting off great. We could talk amongst ourselves AND not have to do any work; THIS was life. Then the news anchor came on, as they were showing the astronauts' preparations to board the shuttle. They were getting ready for the biggest moment of their lives, and the whole world was watching. In the meantime, they were showing background stories of Christa McAuliffe and Ronald McNair. I really connected with her because she was from Boston, and I missed being in Massachusetts. Now the astronauts were walking into the rocket, getting themselves ready for take-off. Once they gave the green light to the command station, they were ready to do the countdown.

10....9....8....7....6....5....4....3....2....1...BLAST OFF.

And they were off. Every one of us in the class was watching in amazement as we were a part of history too. It was crazy watching the shuttle go through the sky, then through the clouds. I was wondering how the people down below felt as they were watching; I bet it was SUPER loud. As onlookers, we were all directing our attention to such an astounding event. Then came an unforeseen tragedy, the shuttle exploded. All you could see were clouds of smoke. "What just happened?" The news people were in disbelief, as we all were. They proceeded to give the grim announcement as tears were welling in their eyes. They stated what was obvious; that the entire shuttle exploded, and there were no known survivors. One minute, we were all excited and gazing at such a historic feat; and the next minute, we were in tears from watching a tragic accident, LIVE. I knew of other people dying, but this was weird seeing this on live television. I guess this is what it sounds like when doves cry because we all shed an extra tear in our hearts that day.

My family had a weird death story just last summer. My Granny's older sister and her husband were found murdered in their house in New Kent. They said it was a murder-suicide. Talk about "till death do us part". My Great Aunt Lucille was found in the kitchen on the floor. She was shot in the head while watching the dishes. And her husband was lying on the bed, with the rifle lying across his chest. Now, of course, the WHOLE family was talking about it. The conspiracy behind it all was baffling to them. The fact that the rifle was found lying across my Great Uncle's chest. How could THAT be? How do you shoot yourself WITH a rifle now and be able to place it on your chest? Yeah, it didn't add up. The buzz amongst the family was that it was their son that did it because he had been dealing with an addiction as well, but that's never been confirmed.

My Granny and her sister were not very close, but they were cordial. I think the thought of this happening to her though, kinda shook her up. I'm sure she thought about her OWN marriage and how this could've been her. But we'll go down that road a little later. Once their arrangements were made, we were making plans to say our "goodbyes." I really didn't know her. I think I'd only met her one time, so THAT should tell you how often my Granny exposed me to certain family members. But nonetheless, we were headed down to the country for the funeral. Granny also had a taste for the "lush life" and made sure she had a few bottles of "Mickey's" and "Miller" beer before we left. Now she varied between those two and sometimes the Heineken brand. We had a fully stocked bar in the basement of our house as well. Booze was always around me growing up.

I can't remember what we were riding in; I think we all piled up in Granny's Monte Carlo. It was Granddaddy, Granny, Baby Joe, Mitchell and me. I believe my sister was there too, but not sure, going off my memory. I remember being at the church which was like the family church herein the country. Everyone in the family that still lived there was in attendance.

And most of our relatives, or extensions thereof, were buried in the back. I remember us walking into the church and how I had on this really cute outfit that was similar to my Cabbage Patch doll. She was wearing a blue dress with a red bow, and I had on a royal blue romper with three red buttons on each shoulder. We were all smelling like fried chicken because Granny made a whole aluminum pan of it, along with a Tupperware bowl of, you know it, potato salad. Granny was looking great. She was stepping in her heels with this really nice dress on and was even wearing a hat if I'm not mistaken. Funny thing was, she HATED anything on her head. All eyes were on us walking in as we walked closer to the casket. I remember seeing her sister lying there, looking lifeless, and how my Granny glanced at her nonchalantly as she turned to walk away.

Baby Joe never liked funerals, so he didn't want to stay. He motioned for me to come with him as we were gonna catch a ride with Cousin Bunny back to my Great Uncle Robert's house where the repass would be. There were so many of our cousins and extended family there. I didn't know everybody, but Baby Joe was like a human Rolodex. He remembered EVERYBODY'S name, how we were related, and introduced me to all of them. My Great Uncle Robert was Granny's brother. He was a bit older, but she would talk about how they were closer in age, and while growing up, she stayed under him and her older brother James. Robert had three daughters and a son. Not only did Granny have a hand in raising them, but many of her nieces and nephews and THEIR children as well. I didn't see many of my cousins often, but I learned a lot from them when in their company or when they visited. While Baby Joe was talking, I had to go to the bathroom; I had to do #2. I'm walking fast, trying to get to the bathroom in Uncle Robert's house. My stomach was bubbling so badly that I had to coax myself the whole way there. "PLEASE let me make it. PLEASE let me make it," I prayed.

Now, I'm going to say this as a disclaimer; this was one of MANY embarrassing moments I've had. Shit, this was the very 1st, so consider yourself family now cause the WHOLE WORLD is about to know. I finally got to the bathroom, and I'm having a hard time getting this romper off. "Shit," I thought, "Why did I put this on anyway?" I had finally broken free, and as I pulled down the romper, the unthinkable happened. I began pooping all over myself. I couldn't hold it. It was piling up in the toilet; oh my gosh. The bad part was I had some on the back of the romper, "How am I gonna get this out?" Then I went to flush the toilet, and it WOULDN'T flush. Now picture this, I'm not home in somebody else's bathroom in the COUNTRY no less with many people around, AND it's only one freaking bathroom in here? Man, I know. I stayed in there for about another 20 minutes, trying to figure out how I was going to make it out of there without anybody knowing I stopped up the toilet.

I walked outside the front door to avoid being seen by anyone out back. It was a good thing I had my Cabbage Patch with me, because she became the shield from the shit stain on my backside. Oh man, looking back now, that was funny as hell. But at that moment, I was mortified. I was standing over to the side of the field by myself, not to be close to anybody who could smell me. My other Uncle Mitchell had called me over to him to tell me something. I looked at his face, all scrunched up. I KNEW he knew. He was like, "Damn, what is that smell?" I said, "I don't know..." and ran the hell off. Then I tried going back over to the spot where I was, only for Baby Joe to motion that we were about to leave.

The whole time I'm thinking, Granny's gonna beat the crap out of me. Luckily for me, Granny had had some more beers and was fucked up. Baby Joe had to help her to the car. We all got to the car, and I was scared to get close. Then Baby Joe said, "What the hell is that smell?" And I was just too embarrassed to hold up my head, "Shawaun, is it you?" he asked. I just shook my head without looking at him. "Damn. Go get some newspapers." Granny looked at me and said, "We'll get you cleaned up when we get to the house."

I liked when Granny was drunk, especially now. She was a lot nicer to people when she was wasted. We were all cramped in the back of the car, and everybody put the windows down. The stench of my behind was on a thousand if there were a Richter scale to judge. They all were in the car with their hands up to their nose the whole way home. I was sitting there feeling shameful, wishing I were somewhere else.

So now, let me get back to my grandparents. They were not the average "cookie-cutter" couple at all. They were volatile at times but maintained the "image" in public. As I got older, Granny told me many stories about her and Granddaddy and how they met. My Granddaddy (Joe Sr.) was fresh out of the Army when she met him at a club called Joneses. Go figure. She was working as a live-in nanny/housekeeper with the Glaser Family. She would tell me she cleaned their house and helped with their two children, JoAnne and Frank. At the time, she was dating another man. I can't remember his name, but that's irrelevant.

Long story short, she ended up being with Joe and dropped the other guy. Now let's get into some details. Granny was a country girl. I mean, a REAL country girl. She was beautiful, don't get me wrong, but she was green to the game and **very** naive. Hell, she's never French kissed a man. She said that was nasty. But she figured out how to do "other" things because she was soon pregnant with Baby Joe.

They were both fortunate to grow up with both parents around, so they had images of marriage around them during their childhood. It may not have been positive imagery, but it was something, unlike many children today who don't have a model at all. They got married on April 21st, 1951, and Baby Joe was born later that year in September. The beginning of their marriage was pretty rocky. There were red flags everywhere, but they grew up in a different era, and there was no such thing as divorce. Listening to her stories and experiencing all that I have, I guess that's why I'm not married yet. Too much bullshit to deal with.

Especially if you're with someone who wasn't about anything in the first place. But I digress; we'll dabble in that area later. They then had three more children; Janice in January, and My Mom, Cheryl, in December of 1954. They are considered Irish twins One being born at the beginning and one at the end of the same year. And last was Mitchell, who was born in October 1958.

Granny was naive for the most part. Granddaddy was from a remote country area as well, but now, he's been cultured from traveling overseas living that army life. From my recollection, Granddaddy got a job in New Hampshire, so they moved north to Massachusetts. Granddaddy would commute to work, and Granny found a few jobs while she was there. She worked at Woolworth's food counter and KLH factory that manufactured speakers. She had a great work ethic and gave 100% everywhere she worked. Many of her superiors entrusted her to manage many roles of responsibility, which wasn't always afforded to many Blacks during that time. These were segregated times, and living in the North offered more benefits, but racial tensions were still prominent. When at Woolworth's, Granny was the cook and cashier. Many customers fell in love with her giving spirit and excellent cooking. She was very proud of the accolades she received but was more enamored by the feelings of "love."

This may seem harmless, but this speaks volumes to the thought concept that would follow my grandmother throughout her life. For her, doing things for others and them loving what she did, was her equation of love and validation. When you've never really been shown love, you will accept fragments in whichever way you can. It became her driving force. The more praise she received, the more love she felt. People can praise you, say kind words, or even honor you somehow, but that doesn't mean it's genuine. This was the 1950s, and as long as you stayed in your place and were a "good nigger", you were treated and rewarded like a pet by its owner.

Back then, whites would "Dangle the carrot," as I would call it. They would give the impression that you were given opportunities, but you only got just enough. In their eyes, you would **never** have more than them; you didn't deserve it. One thing about Granny, though, was that she peeped the game early and realized that she had to outsmart her counterparts at all times. She mastered the role of the "good nigger", but she MOVED like an undercover Boss. She was the shit back then. And like a quiet storm, she didn't realize how powerful she was becoming.

CHAPTER 4

I NEED LOVE

On the weekends, Granny would make a big breakfast. I loved her cooking, and as an adult, I have learned many of those recipes and have perfected them in my way. The spread was enormous. We would have pancakes from scratch, homemade fried potatoes and onions, scrambled eggs, bacon, biscuits, and fatback. It was like buffet heaven. Fatback is hard fat from a mature pig's back that is fried, for those of you who may not know. It's super salty but offers a soft middle with a crunchy, crackling-like top. When you see bags of Cracklings in a chip aisle in a store, you'll know where it's derived from. They grew up eating all kinds of livestock in the country, and sometimes Granny's father would kill them himself to prepare for the family. She would tell me when her father would go out, grab the chickens, cut their heads off, and skin them in boiling water. She said the smell of it all was putrid. But it was one less night of eating just beans and bread.

As tired as she would be, cooking gave her a burst of energy. Knowing that everyone would enjoy what she prepared made it all worth it when completed. I remember we had a room in the house called the breakfast room leading to the kitchen. This was where we ate breakfast, lunch, and dinner. The dining room to the left was only used for special occasions, except for when we watched the floor model TV or when I was playing under the table. Granny would always serve my Granddaddy's plate; first, we little kids, then let her sons make their plates; she always served herself last.

I didn't realize how much I would incorporate these traits in my own life back then. As much as the two of them would argue, I didn't quite understand how she was still so humble to serve him. He always got his plate first at every meal when he was home and waited for her to serve his plate.

Alcohol was a forced motivator for most of my immediate and extended family. And what I mean by that is it was a means to reinvent yourself. If you were meek and mild, it made you loud and courageous. If you were naturally loud, it made you an introvert and paranoid. I visually inhabited all of these emotions throughout my childhood. Years later, Granny talked to me more about her abuse from my Granddaddy. One time he came home; he was already drunk and wanted to beat her up. Because this was going on quite frequently, she decided to beat him at his own game this one time. He provoked an argument while he had another woman sitting outside in the car. They began to wrestle into the hallway of their apartment. She managed to push him down the stairs, and he was screaming for help. He gathered himself and went to the car with the other woman. She set the scene because she didn't have any bruises this time. She proceeded to rip her shirt, mess up her hair more, and then called the police to say that her husband beat her.

Now, this may seem deceptive, but in all actuality, this was a survival move and a bold one at that. Granddaddy was reckless and thought it was ok to treat women any way for your pleasure as if they were your property. That slave mentality runs deep, for real. The police can, and they found him out in the street and arrested my Granddaddy. He was allowed to come back home, but now he knew he could no longer bait the "gentle lamb" with the carrot, for she had become a rampaging bull.

During this time, the school system was changing, and if you didn't get a special request from the School Board, you had to attend the school in your zone. During my last year of elementary, I attended my neighborhood school, A. V. Norrell. It was different because the school was ALL black. Black teachers, administrators, and ALL of the students. No salt in sight. It was kind of cool, though, because now I had gotten a chance to experience kids dealing with issues like me on the low. My teacher was named Ms. Dunlop, and I liked her. She was a young teacher, but you could tell that she loved kids and wanted us to succeed. Many teachers didn't take the time like that, but she reminded me of my teachers in Massachusetts, so I felt at home in her class. Now the kids were a different story. There were kids from all different backgrounds in my class, some worse off than mine. Luckily, one of my childhood friends was in my class. He lived down the street from us with his Mom, sister, little brother, and Grandparents. He spoke of his Dad and how he would come around sometimes, but I don't think his parents were together.

Bo Bo was like my guide in that school, he knew EVERYBODY, and everybody knew him. They knew **not** to mess with him either, or he would beat them up. It's funny; he never treated me that way. Even when we were little kids, he would always come to my Granny's house and play with my drum set in our basement; and he came to my birthday parties thrown by my Mom and Granny in the backyard. My Mom LOVED her some Bo Bo. I think she took to him because she didn't have a son, so she took him like a moth to a flame. While in school I made a few friends, but it was this one girl who didn't like me. She was dark brown-skinned, with a jerry curl, and she always sucked her thumb. She would smile in my face and then do something mean to either get me in trouble or have me hurt myself.

We were having EPAH in the gym, which was our "special" recess day when we did a lot of fun sports-related activities. We were in the gym playing around afterward, and she came over to me and said, "Let's spin."

We then held hands and spun around in a circle. In mid-swing, she let go, and I plummeted to the floor and busted my lip. I'll never forget it was on a Friday.

Every Friday was Granny's "no cooking" day, and my sister and I would get to eat out at McDonald's or Burger King or have pizza. When I fell, she laughed at me, then ran off to not get in trouble. I told Mrs. Dunnlop, and she sent me to the nurse, where I was given ice for my lip. I was so mad when I got home because Granny took us to Burger King, and I couldn't eat my food. The salt from the fries and the ketchup from the burger was burning my lip. My damn weekend was ruined. Monday, I was on a vengeance. I didn't know HOW I would do it, but I was going to get her back.

One problem was that I had never been in a fight before. Hell, I had only three spankings in my life up to this point. I never gave people a problem and never had one come at me where I had to defend myself, but this couldn't go unaddressed. Bo Bo knew what had happened to me, so he was egging me on to hit her the whole day, but I remained cool. Really, I was scared shitless. We were coming from the cafeteria, and Ms. Dunnlop made us form a line to walk down to the class. As we walked, the teacher was ahead of us, so she couldn't see the shenanigans this little girl was doing behind her back. She kept jumping in front of me to try and trip me up in the line, and I was becoming fearful about how I could stop her. As we got closer to the class, my teacher went over to the door to unlock it, and out of nowhere, I swung my blue Rainbow Brite lunch box and hit the little girl in the face. She was stunned. Of course, Bo Bo saw and tried to have us start an all-out brawl. But Ms. Dunnlop heard the commotion behind before the little girl could retaliate.

When we got into the classroom, she made us both stand in front of the room for 5 minutes. And hold hands. It seemed like forever, but that was our punishment and means of apologizing to one another. Ms. Dunnlop already knew that this girl was messing with me and wasn't surprised at my actions.

But she made it a teaching moment for us both, and she never bothered me again. Funny story: the very NEXT year, we attended the same Middle School, Thomas Henderson, and she ran into me outside. I thought she would start some shit again with me, but she wanted to be my friend. She said, "If anybody messes with you, you let me know because I'll fuck um' up for you." The SAME girl that wanted to beat me now would beat anyone that messed with me, that's some karma for you.

A girl had picked on me in 4th grade from Ginter Park that was there with us also. Once I told her, that other girl never looked my way. Man, I'll never forget her. Years later, in my late teens, I saw a story on the news of a girl murdered by her boyfriend and almost fell on the floor when they confirmed it was that same girl who was my oppressor turned rescuer. I couldn't believe it. I began to reminisce about that incident and felt a bit of sadness for her. Those types of stories were becoming commonplace in my neighborhood. Many of the kids I grew up with or went to school with were gone. But this one took a piece of my heart. "Damn." Rest in peace, Pleshette, and thank you for being my protector.

Rap music was going full stream now and all over the airwaves. I loved them all, from Run-DMC to Eric B. & Rakim and Roxanne Shante. My favorite was Whodini. I convinced Granny to buy me their album, and I listened to it all the time. I would sit in my room while listening to the radio and make my tapes. It was hard though, because you always had to make sure you hit pause to cut out the commercials so that you could record the next song uninterrupted.

When this one song came out by LL Cool J, it was unlike anything ever done; it was a love song. Nobody in rap talked about love like that, other than Whodini with their song called "One Love". This talked about an intimate love. At the time, a boy in my class asked me for my number so we could talk after school. I gave him my number because I had a private phone line in my room, so I could be on the phone without disturbing anyone.

We would talk about dumb stuff; hell, we were only around 10 or 11. So there wasn't much of anything going on in MY world with boys. I was still dreaming and playing with dolls. This little boy though had an agenda of his own. He kept saying that he wanted to kiss me, and I would say, "Where on the cheek?"

"Naw girl, on the lips." he would say. He would ask me every day, and I would say no.

When we were talking and his Mom, Cookie would get on the phone and say, "Kevin, get off the phone with this girl and get ready for bed." He would be slightly embarrassed and be like, "C'mon, Mom." At school, he decided to give me a gift. He gave me a rose for Valentine's Day. One afternoon, he called and said he had something he wanted to tell me. He started playing the love song by LL, and that shit stopped me in my tracks. For the very first time, I saw what I was missing, love from a BOY. I was like, "Awwww...this is so sweet. He is so sweet. I think I might kiss him." The next day at school, he sent me a note in class. When I opened it, it had a yes box and a no box, and he asked if I would be his girlfriend. Before I could answer, another girl in my class saw the note and whispered to me, "Don't do it, girl, he sent me one too." And with that lesson, I learned that boys are all talk, sex, and no substance.

Middle school was a perfect time for me. I graduated in the top ten of my elementary school class, so I was excited to move on to bigger things. Middle school, or intermediate school as some call it, was like being in high school, but on a smaller scale. You no longer sat in one classroom or at lunch with the same people every day. Now, you have multiple classes and a crowd of people to have lunch with from multiple classes. Some of you may only see friends on Mondays, Wednesdays, and Fridays. Or it could be on Tuesdays, Wednesdays, or every day of the week, depending on their schedule. Many of my friends from 5th grade came here as well since this was our zone school. Of course, Bo Bo was there with me doing what he did best, causing trouble.

We didn't see each other as much though during school since we had different classes and electives. I decided to take Choir as an elective, being that I was always singing around the house and was in the school chorus in elementary. I loved singing. I loved creating melodies and was a strong soprano back then. I still have a somewhat high-pitched voice, but nowhere near the range I had 25-30 years ago.

On the home front, my Mom was undergoing many changes. Before my 12th birthday, my Mom had another little girl in May. She called me from the hospital and asked what's a good name for her. Luckily, I had a list of names I had created for myself. Since I was always fantasizing, I already had a list of names for a boy or girl when I had kids. I was going down the list of names, and my Mom said, "No, no, no, not that one either". Once I got to the last name on the list, she said, "That's it. That's gonna be her name!" For protection and privacy, I will alter her name a bit. My new sister was named Shaunda Yanae. My Mom sent me pictures of her in the mail. She was so beautiful. She was of mixed race because she was very fair skinned with black hair that had a loose curl.
I couldn't wait to meet her. Now I had another student in my class.

My other sister, Ayana, was now 3 going on 4. The year was 1988, and I still felt inadequate in my skin. I had put on a little more weight, and Granny made me aware of it every chance she got. In 6th grade, I did well and made the scholar roll that first semester. I was super excited. I came home and told Granny, but she didn't seem quite enthused. The teachers had a ceremony every semester to highlight the special academics of those students throughout the 6th grade, called "Student of the Month." The teachers would handpick which students they would honor during the ceremony. Then I would have a special lunch for you and your parents or whoever comes to support you. But they did it in a way where the student never knows until the day of.

My Granny said out of the blue, "I need you to come to the store with me to get a few things." It took me off guard because Granny doesn't usually do stuff like that on a whim. It must be for an event or special occasion. Sometimes she would go **all** out depending on what it is. Last year for Career Day, I did a recorded interview with a local fashion designer and seamstress. The lady, Ms. Deborah, was so lovely. She and her sister ran the business, where she drew sketches, and they both were seamstresses. Because they were so impressed with the interview and my pre-sketches, Granny allowed them to make an outfit for me to wear for Career Day. They also made almost every outfit I needed for special events until I graduated high school. I wonder what happened to them because the storefront shop they occupied downtown closed, and I don't know what happened to those ladies. They were truly great at their craft. Hopefully, somebody who knows them is reading this to let them know that I highlighted their awesome gifts.

That day, I had all eyes on me, struttin' into the school all dressed up. Of course, I got an A+ on the project. But it just shows you how far Granny would go to make sure you were right. Appearances, Appearances. Granny never told me what this outfit was about, but it was super cute. And on that Friday, she told me to put it on. It was peach colored, and the skirt was quite fitted and showed my hips, which I had a lot of at that age and a ruffle at the bottom. And the top was buttoned-down and had a ruffle around the bottom. Then, to top it off, I wrapped a pink bow around my head, accentuating the curls in my Jheri curl.

Yeah, I fell in that hair trap. I forgot to mention how I got a damn Jheri curl in the first place. In 4th grade, I told you Granny would wake me up early to get myself ready for school since she had to be at work before I left. After taking a quick nap after breakfast, I took one last look at myself in the mirror before leaving out.

To me, my ponytail didn't look even, so I proceeded to get the scissors to fix it myself. When finished, my ponytail was even, but it was cut in HALF. I went to school like a proud peacock. And when I got home, Granny saw my head and went OFF. She immediately called Ms. Freda at Harrington's Salon on Brookland Park Blvd. to get my hair done. A neighbor owned the salon a block up the street from us, and she did Granny's hair. When I got that stuff done, I had to walk home with paper towels all around my neck because I was dripping like a cow. The things we go through for beauty. Over time, it got better. Instead of using those awful, juicy activators, I found that Donnie's Coconut cream was way better. I was able to have the curl without the drip.

Ok, so back to where we left off. Now I'm all dressed up in this beautiful peach outfit, ready for school. I got to school, which seemed like a normal day for me. The teachers had all the 6th graders go to the auditorium for the Student of the Month program. Each semester, we looked forward to this day because we never knew who was being nominated. As they would call out a student's name, you would come to the stage, and then your parents would walk out from behind backstage to greet you. Lunch would be set up in a designated room with pizza & refreshments. Then, inductees had the option to leave school early. Everyone is sitting there anticipating whom they will call.

The teachers had called three of my peers and had one name remaining. My math teacher Brenda Corbe said, "And our final Student of The Month recipient is Shawaun Jones." I was SHOCKED. I wasn't expecting this at all. As I walked towards the stage, my Granny came from behind the curtain; all dressed in her fur coat. She knew all along. She was smiling as if she was beaming with pride, and I was so happy to be recognized. That was a special day for me, and the very LAST time Granny ever came to anything I had at school. Then I thought that the only reason she came was so she could shine too. Damn shame if you asked me. But I truly understand it all now. Like Granny would always say when it was something you didn't understand, "Just keep on livin', you'll see."

CHAPTER 5

THE GREATEST LOVE OF ALL

By this time now, my Mom's tribe is growing. I now have two sisters, one living with me and the other living in Massachusetts. It feels like an eternity when I'm not with her. We talk on the phone, but it's not the same as being up under her. My Mom is up there being hella reckless. Ayana and I moved to Virginia because of the lifestyle she was adopting. My new baby sister, Shaunda, was born with cocaine in her system and was put in foster care for the time being. Aunt Janice was doing everything she could to get Shaunda out of there, so she would be with "our" family. As for Cheryl, she is on a downward decline emotionally, mentally, and spiritually. She was having more issues with the law and getting into fights.

One of the fights messed her up real bad. A lady and her husband that my Mom and her siblings grew up with, named Joe Joe, had beat the brakes off my Mom one time. They were all a part of what I could say was a "drugging" crew. They would go to each other's houses or designated locations to get high. They would meet up at our old place, or their place. The lady's name was Paula, and at the time, they had two kids, Taya and Tony. As kids, we became friends since our parents had known each other years prior. I remember they had roaches and mice badly. Sometimes, I would wake up with bite marks on my legs and arms when I stayed over. But when you're getting high, who has time to clean?

Trust me when I say the way that we all lived was like a CPS nightmare story. Our homes were the essence of abuse and neglect, but we managed to stay under the radar of that type of scrutiny. Paula's kids would run around in their underpants most of the time; she didn't care. Although I felt we were different at times, we had a common bond of trauma and addiction surrounding us daily. That's what connected us.

One significant difference was that they got spankings. I wouldn't even categorize it as spankings because they endured straight-up abuse. They would get beat with ANYTHING that would be in reach of Paula to inflict pain. It could be a shoe, a hanger, an extension cord, a belt; you name it; she used it on them. They had a tough life, but we were kids, and kids can be seemingly resilient. It's not until we get older that we see how all that trauma affects you.

Cheryl again found herself expecting, and THIS time it was a boy. I think this excited her. She loved us, but she **always** wanted a boy child. It was so funny. She called me from the hospital to tell me she had him and wanted me to help name him also. I got out my trusty notebook of names, and we named him Darron Lemond. Funny story, though, when they brought him to see her in the hospital room, she denied him at first, saying, "Oh no. That's not MY baby." She said he was dark and had huge eyes; there was **no way** he could be hers. But they assured her that he DID come out of her coochie, and she had to accept him. Man, my Mom was hilarious. She joked about that for the next couple of months.

Since the family had grown, and now my Aunt Janice had my other sister out of foster care, My Mom felt she should move back to Virginia. My Aunt begged her not to go. She said, "Cheryl, don't do it. Stay here. The kids are fine with Momma. There are no opportunities there. Please. I'll help you." But the plea went unnoticed, and she decided to return to Virginia. My grandparents found her an apartment on Chamberlayne Avenue that was pretty nice. I believed my Granddaddy co-signed for her to get the apartment.

It was a cute two-bedroom, one bath townhouse. My Granddaddy even helped to furnish the place. She had a light-colored wood circular dining table for four and a beautiful cream-colored leather sofa. It was so soft; it felt like it swallowed you up like a pillow or cloud until, that is, you began to sweat from sitting too long. Then it would stick to your butt when trying to get up. I convinced my Granny to let me move in with my Mom. I would still be able to go to the same school, and it just so happened that a girl I was friends with when I first moved to Virginia lived in the same complex. Living with my Mom again was great. It felt like we were making up for a lost time.

Having my little siblings around was so fun because I felt like their school teacher. I enjoyed the children's energy and seeing their highs and lows. They could be feeling frustrated, and then you say something to compliment them or give some kudos; their disposition changed immediately. They became exuberant and beaming with pride. They were somewhat hard-headed, but I think that was my Mom's fault. She would go to the store and buy a bunch of small candy and give them each a bag to themselves. Shoot, they were small then, like 1 and 2 years old. It was obvious now that my Mom never really cultivated motherly skills. She meant well, but that's all she knew.

There used to be this girl who lived in the complex to whom I gravitated too. She was a bit older than me, but I was used to being around "grown folk," so it never bothered me. Stephonia was around 25, married, and had two little girls. She was an Army wife and spent most of her time alone with the girls since her husband was constantly deployed or working. She was so beautiful to me. I began to hang out at her house a lot. Or, when she needed to run to the store, I would watch the girls for her. Their names were Samantha and LaTonya. One looked just like her, and the other was a striking resemblance to her husband.

She always talked about how she was going to school but didn't finish because she had started a family. She kept stressing to me, "Girl, no matter what, you better finish school, okay?" I would always nod my head in reply because I valued the passion behind her words and knew that she cared. We spent so much time together; my Mom always knew where I was and sometimes had to come over there to get me to go home. Mainly because she wanted to go out and wanted me to watch the kids.

One day I decided to see Stephonia and walked over to her place in the next building. When I got there, her husband answered the door. It shocked me because I had never met him and only saw pictures of him. "Stephonia went out with the kids, but she's on her way back. You can wait inside until she gets here," he said. He was a slender, nerdy-looking man but somewhat attractive. He reminds me of a nerdy-looking T.I. The rapper from the movie ATL. He seemed nice, if you call a predator nice. For some reason, EVERYTHING in my spirit said: "*No, HELL NO SHAWAUN*", yet I proceeded to walk into the house. I sat down on the sofa, farthest away from him, when I walked in. He looked at me with googly eyes as if we wanted to bite the forbidden apple. I felt kinda weird but appeared unafraid outwardly. He asked if I wanted anything to drink, and I politely declined. He then sat in the chair right by the sofa while staring. By this time, the level of comfort was gone. And my spidey senses kept telling me, "*Shawaun, get the hell out of here NOW.*"

I said to him, "Well, I'm gonna go. Just let Stephonia know that I came by and will come back later."

"Oh no, you should wait for her. She will be back any minute," he said.

Again, I went against my intuition, hoping that what I was feeling was completely off. He then sat on the sofa on the opposite end and motioned me to slide down. I inched a bit closer but was too afraid to oblige anymore. He then moved closer to me and began to touch my breast. As I said, I was physically shapely and built like a woman at a very early age.

My Mom was very top-heavy, and I was blessed with a C cup by the time I was 13. While touching me, I KNEW this was wrong, although it felt good. I began having a battle in my mind, "Should I have him stop? This isn't right. Make him stop." I tried to get up, and he grabbed me and set me back down. His grip became intense as he groped me and tried to get on top of me.

I kept saying, "No. No. Stop. This isn't right." And since he ignored my plea, I began to fight back with even MORE resistance.

He kept saying, "Stop fighting me. You KNOW you want it." He was very strong for such a small-framed man. But I couldn't stop. I knew if I did, he would conquer me. I finally managed to get from his clutch and ran out of there fast. That day I learned how to depend on myself. There was no way I could ever go back over there now. About a week or so later, I saw Stephonia and another girl walking toward my house. My Mom and I were in the living room watching tv. She started yelling, saying, "Shawaun, get your ass out here. You wanna be grown, huh? Get your ass out here so I can BEAT you like you're grown." Now, I hadn't told my Mom what I experienced the last time I was there. But the way she was reacting, my Mom knew something had gone down. And that somebody was lying. I had never really cursed out in the open before, let alone around my Mom. I was respectful like that. But this seemed as good a time as any to break that rule of thumb. It was better to ask for forgiveness than permission at this moment. So I began the tit-for-tat banter with this grown-ass woman.

Here she is, 25, and I'm 13. The more she kept going, I knew what this was about, her husband lied. My Mom didn't have a CLUE as to what happened, but she soon realized what had transpired. "I didn't do anything. Why the hell are you here?" "Oh, you KNOW why I'm here bitch.. You couldn't keep your hands off my man." she said. My Mom looked at me and could see the look of innocence on my face.

She went to open the door, and Stephonia tried to push her way in. Now my Mom was 5'9", and about 245 at the time, so this girl was not getting in. Hell, she was shorter than me and tiny in size. She continued yelling obscenities, causing a scene in the parking lot in front of our place. On the other hand, I was so nervous and mad simultaneously that I began shaking from all the commotion.

The neighbors began to come outside to see all the fuss going on. My Mom was still at the door, trying forcefully to keep Stephonia out. She put her foot in the door to edge her way in. But the strength of my Mom's force had her foot beginning to look like a pancake. She finally moved her foot from the door and walked off limping, still yelling at me and calling me names. It was then that I told my Mom EVERYTHING that went down. She had a look of sadness but concern at the same time. Then, she gave me "the talk" and damned near told me EVERYTHING about sex. From how it may feel, to how to buy condoms, how to keep the area clean, to what it could mean if my coochie began to smell like she left NO stone unturned. I felt overwhelmed by all the information because sex was the farthest from my mind then. I didn't want to give up my virginity yet, although many girls my age at school already had. I knew that wasn't for me.

Sad to say, but about a week after the incident, I was walking from the school bus heading to the house, and I saw Stephonia walking in the opposite direction, alone. Her face had been beaten to a pulp. The whole left side was reddish-black and accentuated the black eye. I felt so bad for her. We managed to glance at each other, and all the words spoken outside my door that day seemed to be forgotten. She was almost afraid to look at me long, but her expression spoke volumes.

Later in my life, I ran into that guy again, twice. The first time I was about 17, I believe he followed me and found out where my grandmother lived. I was walking from the store, and he was walking behind me down the block.
"Hey, it's good to see you. How have you been? Can I call you sometime?"

And to not make too much conversation, I politely said, "No, I can't have phone calls."

"Well, can I take you out to lunch one day after school? Or can I take you out shopping for some new tennis shoes? Would you like that?" he said. I walked even faster and said, "No, that's okay. I'm fine without that." The faster I walked, the more he picked up speed. Luckily, a neighbor came out of the house and noticed our interaction. I guess it looked apparent that I was uncomfortable, so the neighbor yelled out, "How you doing today, Sweetie." and I replied, "Fine, Ma'am." seeing that he may be approached, he then said, "Okay, then, hopefully, you will find me so I can take care of you." The way HE cared for women? I wanted NO part of that.

The second time, I had my third daughter by then. I was between being single and having a friend with benefits. I was bored, so I decided to open an online dating profile, and guess who spotted me out? I wanted to ignore the request, but my spirit said, "Talk to him and END this once and for all." So I had a backup number that I gave him to call. We talked, and he asked me about myself, and I asked if he had kids.

"Yes, I have two girls. One is 26, and one is 24. My oldest is about to get married." I asked him if his daughters were named Samantha and Latonya, and he said, "Yeah, you know my daughters?" Immediately I said to myself, "This nigga doesn't remember me at all." I took this as an opportunity to speak my peace to end this saga.

"Were you married to someone named Stephonia?" I then said, "Look, I remember you CLEARLY. I was 13 years old, and you tried to violate me. You were a grown-ass man with a wife AND kids. I only accepted your request because I wanted to tell you that what you did fucked me up. Don't ever reach out to me again." And with that, I closed that chapter of my life.

My Mom began dating this guy named Robert; he had a daughter that was deaf. She wore a hearing aid, but was extremely pretty. She also attended my school. She was a year younger than me but was considered "special", according to the school's label. I admired her hazel eyes; they were beautiful and matched her bright smile. He and his daughter began coming over to the house more often. Our parents would go out and then come back and he would pick up his daughter. In the beginning, I liked how he presented himself. He was very respectful and seemed very kind. I loved the way he treated his daughter like a little princess. It made me wonder what it would be like if I had a Dad to treat me that way. Over time though, He would come over smelling like alcohol, and I knew then that this nigga was like ALL the rest, another john getting some ass. Soon after, he stopped coming over, and my Mom introduced me to another man who lived down the street.

My Mom said she would help him sometimes since he could not come in and out due to his health. One day, we visited him and walked down Chamberlayne to his apartment building. This is the same building my Uncle Mitchell would get an apartment not long after. We rang the bell at the door, and he buzzed us in. We walked in, and it smelled of antiseptic, like in a hospital. We turned to the left, and this man was sitting on the edge of the bed. This man was well over 500 lbs. I had never seen anyone that large up close. But he could barely get around at all. And my Mom began cleaning some of the areas around him. "Hi. How are you, little girl?" he said. "I'm fine," I said. He and my Mom began a light conversation, and I zoned out. I was thinking in my mind, "What in the world? I HOPE she is not having sex with him. HOW could she? I wonder how he even goes to the bathroom." As I was in my daze, my Mom broke my trance and said, "C'mon, let's get ready to go." The man, named Leroy, said his goodbyes as we walked out the door. I wanted to ask my Mom about this man and the nature of their relationship, but I didn't want to pry. It was none of my business anyway. But just the THOUGHT of what was going on made me sick.

It was that time of year again for Miss. Princess pageant at school. Each year, girls would prepare for this event. It was set up like a real pageant. You had to perform some talent, and then you had to model a beautiful gown and answer whatever question the judges asked, followed by your final walk on stage before announcing the winner. This year, I wanted to break out of my comfort zone and participate. Last year, a girl named Nevea Peterson won. She could sing. She was in the choir with me, and was running again this time. I was nervous since she was my competition, but I was determined to outshine her. "Everybody knows she can sing. Let someone else shine." I thought as I was preparing for the event. I convinced Granny to get me a dress for the pageant; it was Magenta colored and had a ruffle at the bottom with shoulder straps. I thought I looked nice in it. I wanted to get another dress to have one to perform in and one to have my final walk-in. I decided to sing Whitney Houston's "The Greatest Love of All" as my selected choice to perform.

I practiced every day at home, trying to show that Nevea wasn't the ONLY one who could sing. On the day of the pageant, I was super nervous. I ended up not being able to get a dress, so I had to wear the pink one twice, which frustrated me. It was time for me to get on stage to perform my song. I was nervous as hell, and the stage fright was increasingly growing. The music started, and all I could see were the faces in the crowd looking at me. I was petrified. And low and below, my Mom walked in with my little sister and brother in the stroller and some flowers in her hand. They were a bit of a distraction to the crowd since the lights had been dimmed, and when the door opened, the light was shining through when I saw her give me the nod and dare to belt out the song. I didn't think I was that good, and my voice was so shaky from fear, but I got through it. When done, some of the kids stood and clapped for me to show me support for pushing past my fear. I was pretty shy when it came to forging out on my own, but in the choir, I was LOUD and unforgiving.

Two other people performed, and then Nevea was set to go up last. To my surprise, she ended up singing the SAME damn song. At that point, I KNEW I had lost because she killed that song. By this point, I didn't even want to come back on stage for the final walk, but I did. They announced Nevea Peterson as the 7th Grade winner of the Miss. Princess pageant and the whole crowd began to cheer. I just stood there feeling embarrassed once again. Feeling as if my voice didn't compare to hers. How we learn to perceive ourselves can be a trip in itself. Once I got to my Mom, she hugged me and said, You did well up there. I'm so proud of you." That was the first time in a while that I received any validation, especially from my Mom. I was glad someone was there to encourage me because I needed that safety net of love. The teachers allowed me to leave school early that day; I was glad it was all over.

I loved that my Mom had cable because Granny only had the regular local channels. So I watched so many movies that I usually wouldn't have the opportunity to look at. Even the nasty ones back then that came on HBO and Cinemax. The porn was like my entrance to the world of sex in plain sight. Yes, I knew my Mom had had multiple partners, but I never saw it. Except when I was about 6 or 7, I had fallen asleep on the sofa, woke up, and saw that my bedroom door was closed. I wanted to get something out of my room, and when I opened the door, I saw my Mom with her legs wide open and this man "Feasting" on her coochie. I immediately closed the door. She saw me, but she didn't have him stop, and he was too engulfed in what he was doing. So yeah, I had already had some taste of what sex was about visually.

I watched a movie called *The Serpent and The Rainbow* that aired on HBO. It freaked me out. It was based on a true story about a doctor in California who had heard about this potion in the Islands that caused your bodily organs to shut down temporarily, but you would still have all of your senses; but wouldn't be able to move or speak.

In the movie, the man went to the islands, began questioning some of the natives, and was sprinkled with the dust that put him in this state. The voodoo man had him buried alive with a tarantula spider in the casket to get rid of him. The coffin had a glass cross opening in the top so that he could watch them pour the dirt on him. Man, this movie had me SHOOK, let me tell you. I began thinking more about death and how I didn't want to die. My Mom was coming down the stairs and came and sat beside me on the sofa. She was very solemn and somewhat expressionless.

I asked, "Why do we have to die?" At first, she looked and wasn't sure how to answer, but then she replied, "We all have to go one day; it's just a part of life, I guess."

"Well, I don't WANT to go. I want to stay here, see everything, and not miss anyone." She then looked at me with seriousness in her eyes.

"I've had dreams about the police again." Whenever my Mom had these dreams, something bad soon followed. Either she would be in a fight, or a huge argument, have money stolen, or even be arrested; you just never knew.

"I don't know what's going to happen, but I want you to promise me that whatever it is, you're not gonna cry," she said. So now I'm sitting there like, "Where is this coming from?" And she saw the look on my face and repeated, "Promise me you won't cry?" I looked with reassurance and said, "Okay, I promise." If only I had known then how precious time is, I would've prepared myself better for what was to come.

CHAPTER 6

NO MORE FAIRY TALES

September was rolling around again, and it was back to school time. I was about to start the 9th grade, and I was excited about high school. I had the opportunity to go to the newly created Magnet school for the Arts. Since elementary, I had been with most of the kids, and I wanted to see some fresh new faces. So I opted not to go to the zone school where everyone would be. I went to a Southside school to meet new people, and see new faces. A handful of us came along from my school, so I didn't feel entirely alone. I believe it was 4 of us all together, coming from Henderson, and I was ready. Now I had to adjust to an even LARGER environment as I did at the start of middle school. These kids looked like grown-ups to me, but they were students. Most of us began our own "cliques" that we hung out with. Our 9th-grade class was separated into three parts.

You had the General Ed students, the Magnet students, and the Kenan students. The Kenan students were the elite class. They had maintained 3.2 or better grade point averages, so they were at the top of the food chain. The Magnet students were in the middle. We were afforded many opportunities to explore many facets of the Performing and Visual Arts since this was the first pilot program ever of its kind in Richmond Public Schools. It was exciting to be a part of history, the first Magnet group. Of course, on the home front, things began to normalize some.

After the incident with Stephonia, I had to move back to my Granny's house. My Granny never really trusted me after that, I don't think. She constantly accused me of doing stuff with boys that I wasn't. I remember that during that time, I hadn't even started my menstrual cycle yet, and most of my friends had already. I was looking forward to swapping stories with my girlfriends about cramps. One problem I did have was that I would have the worst yeast infections. Sorry to get so personal, but hey, I want you to know ALL of me.

I kept telling my Granny that I was having issues down there, and she then made an appointment for me to see the pediatrician Dr. Cynthia Loone. Dr. Loone accepted Medicaid insurance, which was given to low-income families for affordable medical care. Her office STAYED packed. Sometimes you would have to wait 3-5 hours just to be seen, and she had many patients. She performed my very first gynecological exam. During the visit, I told her my issues and explained that I wasn't sexually active but couldn't get rid of the infection. She did the exam and then said we would have some results as early as the end of the week because the lab was backed up.

So Granny and I left to await the news on how to proceed. My Mom would bring Shaunda and Darron over on the weekends when I was out of school so Ayana and I could spend time with them. When they would come over, though, it was as if they couldn't touch anything of Ayana's without her having a fit. She did not let them play with her stuff and would tell my Granny if they did. Granny would then get Ayana's old, broken toys to give them to play with. I thought that was pretty shady at times, so when they weren't looking, I would swap out the toys and play with them so they wouldn't get into trouble.

The call finally came in with my results from Dr. Loone. My Granny took the call and was listening intently. "Yes, I understand. I will come to pick up the prescription later today," she said. She looked at me with disgust and said, "Your nasty ass out here being grown. THAT'S the reason for all of this."

"What are you talking about, Granny?" I said with a bit of attitude and sarcasm.

"That's why your ass got Gonorrhea. Dr. Loone just told me." I'm sitting there thinking to myself, "She's lying. How could that be? Isn't that a sexually transmitted disease? I would have to be having sex to have that."

"Granny, I'm NOT having sex. I've NEVER had sex. That test is wrong." I replied.

"It ain't no damn lie. And the test proves it." she responded. At that moment, I felt like I was paying for the sins of my mother. I was like my Mom's twin. But the way Granny talked to me made me feel like she would never change her view of me from that moment on. I felt dirty and shameful for something I wasn't even doing in the first place. It was only the beginning of the heartache I would feel. No more living life in my own paradise or fairy tales. Felt like life was going in a downward spiral of disaster.

November was here, and Granny was preparing early this year for Thanksgiving. We had a huge deep freezer in the basement, where she put the turkey and ham for her to prepare for the holiday. I was watching "The Geraldo Show" after school. I liked how he would be direct with the guests on stage and wasn't afraid to talk about tough subjects. My Mom had called, and I asked, "When are y'all coming over? Are you on the way?" "Yeah, I'm waiting for Deiddy to pick us up." My Mom and her siblings called my Granddaddy, a slang and country way of saying Daddy. When he arrived at her house, she called me back to say they were leaving, and she was on the way.

I was so looking forward to seeing her. I looked forward to when she would come by during the week for a few hours with the kids. I was wondering what was taking them so long to get here. Her place on Chamberlayne Avenue, which was not that far from Granny's house on Edgewood Avenue; so I couldn't imagine the delay.

"I wish they would hurry up." I thought to myself. Not long after Granny came home, and the phone began to ring. An hour had passed since my Mom had called, so I thought it was her. She answered, and her eyes widened in disbelief as if whatever she was hearing was startling news. When she put the phone down, she took a deep breath to collect herself, looked at me, and said, "C'mon, we gotta go to the hospital, it's Cheryl."

My heart was now in my throat with worry and fear about what had happened. I couldn't imagine what could be wrong. I had **just** talked to her. She was on her way there. Immediately, I began to blame myself for whatever had happened. "If I hadn't rushed her to get here, this wouldn't have happened." Baby Joe was there in the waiting room with Granddaddy and the kids at the hospital. Granny told him to take the kids home, and she wanted me to go with them, but I refused; I HAD to be there with my Mom. Baby Joe began giving the play-by-play of what had happened because he saw it all. My Uncle and some of his friends were sitting on the steps of the house on the corner of Edgewood Avenue and Brookland Park Blvd. facing the corner store R & S. My Granddaddy had pulled up his car right alongside where they were sitting so that my Mom could get out and walk over to the store.

"Are you going to the house?" Baby Joe yelled out to my Mom.

She walked over to him, "Yeah, I'm gonna stay for a while, see Shawaun for a few hours, then go back home. I'm just going to get some cigs first."

"All right then," he replied, and my Mom proceeded to walk across the street. It's a residential area, for the most part, so the speed limit is around 35 mph on the main road and 25 mph on the side streets. My Mom got to the middle of the road by the double yellow lines, waiting for the cars to go by so she could cross. My Uncle said you could hear a revving sound coming closer down the street, it was a motorcycle going at least 60 miles per hour up Brookland Park.

As soon as my Mom began to step toward the store, the motorcycle's speed was too fast for the driver to slow down, and he hit my Mom. She flipped in the air and plummeted to the ground face-first. The biker fell off the bike, and the motorcycle skidded down the street for another block. Everyone around was in shock and disbelief at what had just happened. Baby Joe and his friends were standing there like, "Oh shit". My siblings were in the backseat of my Granddaddy's car, viewing our Mom on the ground. At the time, they were only 2 and 3 years old.

They looked at our Mom on the ground, motionless. The bystanders thought my Mom was dead and didn't want to touch her. The Asian guy who owned and operated the store, came out and ran to my Mom on the ground to see if he could find a pulse. He yelled, "Call 911. Get the ambulance now." People were still just standing around looking at my Mom on the ground. Baby Joe walked over to her and said her right eye was hanging out of the socket beside her. The store owner then began to cut her clothes off so that they would be able to treat her quickly when the ambulance came. My Mom lay on the hard concrete for about 5-8 minutes before the ambulance showed up, naked and exposed. In that moment, I know it seemed like an eternity. She was then rushed to MCV hospital, where we were waiting to hear from a doctor. The picture Baby Joe painted was so typical of any other story I've heard him tell. It was vivid; I felt like I had seen the entire incident and was nowhere near the scene. The funny thing was, I was rushing her to get to my Granny's, not knowing she was fighting for her life just three blocks away from me.

While we were sitting in the small waiting room, this man came storming into the hospital, yelling, "Where's Shirley? Where is Shirley?" He was escorted by a Security Guard while yelling in the hospital hallway. "Did he mean Cheryl?" I thought. But at the time, his interruption still couldn't cut through the thick silence that took over the room. Finally, one of the operating doctors came in.

He stated that my Mom was struck by the motorcycle and suffered from two broken arms, legs and had suffered brain damage. Currently, fluid was swelling up her brain, and they needed to do a procedure to drain it so that she could live. He stated that the procedure had only been done twice in the U.S., and she would have a 50/50 chance of survival. Hearing those words made me feel even worse. "Why did I rush her to come over? I should've told her to wait until the weekend."

Granny decided to sign off on the procedure, and the doctors were underway. We waited for another 3 hours before they allowed us to see her. My Granddaddy had left with the kids while Baby Joe, my Granny, and I remained. When they gave us the ok to see her, I wasn't sure what to expect. We walked into the room, and she was lying on the bed with all these tubes hooked up to her. One of them was coming out of the top of her head. She was unrecognizable. The trauma from the accident had her face black and blue, and her body was swollen 3x the size. I looked at her in disbelief. I thought to myself, "This can't be Cheryl? This can't be Cheryl? She can't die on me. She HAS to live."

The next couple of weeks were rocky at best. As a family, we were dealing with the transition. My mother was now in a coma, and we were anticipating her awakening. My two younger siblings are now living with us too, so we all had to adjust to that. Granny was steadily putting things in place, going from raising two of her grandchildren to now all four. In school, I just couldn't function like before. I would physically be there, but my mind was somewhere else. It was as if my mind was on constant replay of it all. I still couldn't imagine that this was my life right now. After school, Granny and I went to the hospital. My sister Ayana came as well, but the other two were too young. I remember walking in and seeing all of the machines around her. She needed machines to help her breathe, monitor her heart, drain more fluid, and check her pressure levels. It looked like a picture of despair. Granny would go by her bedside to touch her hand and say, "Cheryl, we're all here." It felt so cold and empty in there, although machines surrounded us. We all just kind of stood around, and the nurse came over and said, "You can talk to her. She may be in a coma, but she can hear you." That was a green light for me. I wanted her to hear me and KNOW that I was right by her side. I walked over to the bed and held her hand. "Cheryl, it's me, it's Shawaun; I'm here with you."

When I said that, it was as if the atmosphere had shifted. She tightened her grip on my hand, and you could see her mouthing my name, "Sha-wa-un," but there was no sound. When I saw this, I immediately wanted to cry. But my mind took me back to the day we talked about death and how she felt something would happen, and I promised not to cry. Omg, that recollection hit me like a ton of bricks. She knew this was going to happen. When we left, I kept replaying that conversation on her sofa, and the last time we talked that day, she was on her way over to Granny's. I couldn't stop repeating over and over in my head the words she spoke, "Promise me you won't cry…Promise me you won't cry."

Every time we would go to the hospital now; it was like clockwork. Granny or someone would say they were in the room, and Cheryl just laid there. But as soon as I said I was there, she did the same thing every time…. she mouthed my name. I never boasted or bragged about it with my family. I just looked at that as a testament to the connection that my Mom and I had. It didn't matter what obstacle was between us; we would always manage to stay connected. I'm sure it was a change for her, as it was for us. After three long weeks in a coma, Cheryl had awakened to what was now her new reality.

While she was undergoing some new realities, so was I. I had just turned 14 and was looking like I was 18. Granny had given me a few inches to roam off the leash she had me on, so I made sure to utilize it wisely and as often as I could. I would always walk through Battery Park to Burger King on Chamberlayne Avenue. It was a nice little walk and allowed me some time to myself. This guy I would always admire from afar worked at that location. He was tall and had beautiful hazel eyes. I was mesmerized by his eyes and how he looked at me. I was going up there just about every day. We would glance at each other, and he would wink at me while working. He was like my first real crush. I finally got the opportunity to talk to him one day.

He came from the back to get the trash and saw me sitting in a booth, so he came over. "I see you come in here all the time; what's your name?" he asked. "My name is Shawaun, and yours?" "My name is Kevin; nice to meet you." And from then on, we formed what I considered a friendship. Everyday after school, I would walk to Burger King so I could see Kevin. My heart would flutter whenever I was around him. I felt all giddy inside. One day, he caught me off guard while we were outside talking. I was in mid-conversation when he leaned over and kissed me. I didn't know how to take it at first. It was slow and soft, and I felt a little weak after. This was my very first kiss. I lost contact with him after that, and he stopped working there. I missed the thrill of seeing him, but he opened a door that could no longer stay closed.

Over the summer, I met another boy through a friend; his name was Christian. He and I clicked immediately. We would talk on the phone for hours at a time. Since we lived on different sides of town, we spoke of our community environment. He had an older sister named Shari, and she would be yelling at him a lot in the background. His Mom was always so nice to me. I remember when we first met. We talked on the phone for a few weeks and decided to meet up at the park down the street from me. I remember when I saw him, in my mind, I was like, "Oh wow. He looks NOTHING like how I imagined. I hope he doesn't expect me to kiss him." Omg, if he ever reads this, he's going to flip. I can say that boy turned into a great man and has been a genuine friend for over 30 years. He's not just some "boy" I met at 14; he's family to me now. We've lost contact a few times over the years, but whenever I need him, he's always there. Big ups to you, OG. Thank you for being genuine; I honor you.

By now, Cheryl was doing a lot better. The doctors suggested that she go for rehab and therapy at Sheltering Arms Rehabilitation in Richmond. I would visit just about every day during her therapy sessions to give her moral support. She had to learn how to do everything all over again. They were teaching her how to get up out of bed, how to push herself into a standing position, as well as how to communicate. They used various devices, and she had to learn to write with her left hand, being that she was originally right-handed. The whole process was slow but promisingly progressive. The legalities behind it all were putting a strain on Granny on the home front. She sought legal advice on the matter from one of her clients, Sara Fielders. I told you Granny was a domestic and introduced us to many of her clients over the years.

This particular client had been with her since she graduated college. She was a lawyer and assisted Granny with any legal situations, often free of charge. Granny seemed to love her, but I was always skeptical of her. Not to seem racist, but she was like an undercover bigot to me. She praised Granny for keeping her house clean for her and her family, and by right, Granny loved to do it.

That was her exchange and has been throughout her life. But if Granny ever got anything materialistic or wanted to do anything to progress herself, this Lady always found an issue with it. She would even tell her that she was doing too much for her grandkids. I look at it this way; if Granny HADN'T done anything for us, I can only IMAGINE where we would've ended up. Her struggles and mishaps were unlike ours. Sara became a tremendous resource for Granny, and at times, us as well.

In school, I was getting accustomed to experiencing all the facets of the arts. I loved it, to be quite honest. It allowed me to develop more knowledge in each area and even find ways to mesh them together. I had a knack for singing and now was working on my range and tone. My teachers, Mrs. Anderson and Mrs. Wooldridge were a tag team for voice training. They each provided me with different techniques to help push out the correct sound and create the proper tone and pitch. They taught a lot about the formation of words when singing. Some words spoken in conversation cannot be pronounced or enunciated the same way while singing. It makes for a balanced sound or a dry vibration.

The art class was perfect for me, also. I would dabble at home, drawing random stuff, and I was pretty good if I said so myself. It helped to formulate my creative niches that were brewing inside. My art expresses more realism through shadowing and abstract art designs. My dance teacher, Ms. Hodel, was cool. I never considered myself a dancer, but I realize now that dance is an expression of freedom. It can show both beauty and strength as our bodies masterfully move to their cosmic rhythms.

Back then, I had no clue what freedom was, let alone what it felt like; so her class always seemed "fake" to me. I felt like I was pretending when I wanted to bask in that feeling in real life. Another class we had in the Magnet program was the drama class. Ms. Huffman was an incredible display of what magnetic energy looked like on and off stage.

Her demeanor was so colorful that you couldn't help but love her. A lot of what I was learning in the choir helped me in this class. It's funny how they intertwine. Ms. Huffman gave us all an opportunity to showcase our hidden talents through acting and a childhood dream of mine.

In my mind I was fearless and unstoppable, but in reality; I was the complete opposite. I was afraid for people to see the "real" me. I believed that part of myself was dirty, unworthy, and insignificant. I would only be as good as what I was able to do for someone else and be validated by that. Sounds crazy, right? But I felt that way. Whenever I believed that I was knowledgeable about something, my family said I was "stupid" or "nobody cares about that", especially my Granny. Words can have such a powerful effect on the human psyche. At school, I learned to be one way and someone different at home. This was the beginning of my "double life."

CHAPTER 7

DREAM ON DREAMER

Some time had passed, and my Mom's condition hadn't improved. She was doing so well at Sheltering Arms and was making such progress, but reality hit. The state was no longer going to fund her care, and the bike driver had filed for bankruptcy, so it seemed out of our hands. Granny, at the time, didn't know what the next steps would be best moving forward. They offered to send her to Wytheville, VA, to a facility called Woodrow Wilson Rehabilitation Ctr. It was a pretty good distance away from us, and Granny didn't want to be that far away. So, the worst-case scenario happened, and we had to put her in a nursing home. For a while, it didn't seem bad. She got up every day, did activities, and got to know a lot of the residents and workers at the facility. Unlike the previous facility, which was within walking distance; that didn't keep me from seeing her on a regular basis.

I should add that the nursing home was not in the best of areas. Cool Lane, where the home was, was smack dab in the middle of two of the worst housing projects. Whitcomb and Fairfield Courts were two of the most notorious on the East side of town. You did **not** want to be down there any time after dark. That's when the fireworks and light show of gunfire began. I would still make it a point to go as often as possible. It mattered to me that the staff knew she had family visiting. I had watched so many other patients being mistreated because they knew no one was ever coming to see them. I'd be damned if they were going to mistreat my mother. I refused to stand by and let that happen.

It was nearing the end of my Junior year and would soon be graduating. It still seems like yesterday that this roller coaster ride began. Things at home were topsy-turvy, almost as if the house was divided somehow. About a year ago, for Mother's Day, my Aunt Janice came down to visit. She never came that often anyway, so it was good to see her and spend time with her. She hoovered a lot over Shaunda and spent extra time with her than the rest of us. For some reason, a color war began between my younger sisters. Ayana was light brown in complexion, similar to caramel, and Shaunda was like "high yellow" with beautiful hair. Let me stop and say this real quick. As Blacks, African Americans, or whatever you want to call us, we've become "conditioned" to degrade our own.

History shows that during slavery, the fairer skinned slaves received better treatment. And the darker the skin, the greater the punishment. Those same ideologies were being perpetrated right in front of my eyes. They were kids, they didn't know any better. In their mind, they were sisters. But the distorted mindsets of the older adults, and so many other outside influences, made it personal, a competition even. Shaunda always had to try to be better than Ayana. In my Granny's eyes, Ayana was "her" baby, and could do no wrong. I saw the injustices being played out against all my younger siblings. They were like the oddballs out. For a while, I defended them. Over time though, I became an accomplice and inflicted the same pain. Monkey see, monkey do.

My Aunt gravitated more towards her because she had a hand in raising her after leaving the foster home, prior to my Mom coming back to Virginia. I can't remember if we were going somewhere or not, but Granny had told me to put a particular dress on Shaunda. The dress was kinda short and looked as if she had outgrown it. My Aunt had a fit when she saw it and said, "Why did you put that on her. Take it off."
"Granny told me to put it on her." I replied. She then voiced her thoughts aloud, "I don't know why Moma said that. This dress is way too short. I'm going to find her something else."
Granny had walked past and overheard what was said as she was speaking. She turned around and said, "What's wrong with the dress? Ain't nothing wrong with it; she looks fine."

"Moma, this dress is too short for her. Doesn't she have something else to put on?" my Aunt said.

"What she has on is FINE. Ain't nothing wrong with that dress." The two of them began to battle it out in a verbal debate over this dress. Then Granny had the nerve to say, "Look, I don't know why you came trying to run things. Cheryl doesn't want you here anyway." My thought was, "How the hell do YOU know what my mother wants. You barely say a word when we see her." She continued to say stuff about my Mom, and I could feel this anger swelling up inside me. I began to yell, "DON'T TALK ABOUT MY MOM. How do you know what she wants anyway?" "You shut up. I'm not talking to you. Stay out of grown folks' conversation."

The more she talked, the madder I got. I had a cup of juice in my hand, and just like in 5th grade, when Pleshette tried to cut the line, without realizing the cup became the lunch bag, and I threw the drink in my Granny's face. Boy, I had NEVER done anything so bold in ALL my days. But I wasn't going to let ANYBODY disrespect my Mom. Especially with her not being there to defend herself. Once the initial shock wore off, instantly, she took her heavy hand and back-slapped me in the face. The taste of blood came inside my mouth, and I went to touch my face and saw blood. Granny stormed out of the room into her bedroom, yelling, "I wish you would just go back to Massachusetts. Don't nobody want you here anyway." My Aunt was low-key heartbroken and mumbled, "This is why I don't come to Virginia. It will be a long time before I ever come back again." She then called my Granny's younger sister, my Great Aunt Teeny, and celebrated Mother's Day with her. What a slap in the face that must've been for my Granny's daughter to spend mother's day without her mother. This was a real turning point in their relationship, and it wasn't a good one. As for me, it was just another lonely day without my Mom.

I had to find a way to get away from it all. Away from the craziness called "my family" and onto somewhere peaceful. I thought about going off to college to escape this madness but knew money would be a massive barrier for that to happen. I was okay in school academically, but I wasn't like the Kenan kids, who were extra smart. Don't get me wrong, I made decent grades; but my attendance sucked. I had missed so many days and had so many tardies that it affected my overall look of being a model student for college. I had to do something; I just didn't know what. Every year, we had something like a spirit week called "Kaleidoscope Week" for Homecoming. The school would schedule all kinds of activities for the student body to do and held an art contest. You would have to draw something that represented what Kaleidoscope week meant to you, and you would either win a cash prize or something else.

This year, the winner could receive a cash prize of $25 or a ticket to the upcoming MC Hammer concert. So I decided to stab it, I mean, "What would it hurt anyway? On the day of announcing the winner, I was in homeroom waiting for the bell to ring. My next class was Algebra I, which was downstairs. I liked my teacher Mr. Jones, especially since we had the same last name. He had a way of making me think outside the box and apply it to my daily life. It helped me to see the world through a whole different lens.

Listening to the latest school news and different upcoming events for the week, I didn't think I would win. So many other bonafide artists had submitted entries as well. "And the winner of the Kaleidoscope art contest is…Shawaun Jones. Congratulations Shawaun. Your artwork will be featured on all of our flyers for this week's event around the school. Please see Mrs. Aggert in the art room as soon as possible to discuss your choice of the prize." I was SHOCKED to hear my name. I couldn't believe it. All of my classmates congratulated me on winning. Some even came directly to me and said, "Congratulations, Girl." I was beaming with pride on the inside as I walked to my next class.

While walking down the hall, I had one of my peers named, Twiggy stop me. We all called him Twiggy, because he was so tall and slim in stature. "Congratulations, Shawaun. How did you win anyway? I didn't think you could draw like that. Didn't you copy that idea from somewhere else?" I was somewhat taken aback by the "assumption" that I had no drawing ability or the decency to win fairly. "Thanks, Twiggy. Well, I guess my design was enough to win though huh." That moment solidified so much of what I would learn later in life. People may smile with you, but that doesn't mean they are happy FOR you. It took me a while to appreciate and accept that even those who may spite you are necessary elements to your growth. These are the same people who help to propel you forward. Just don't allow their adverse energy to take root in your spirit. That's when you relinquish your power to them, which I encountered many times.

That same year, Mrs. Rivers had me participate in a sorority pageant, where I had one of my good friends from school escort me. We had the same last name and used to joke around that we were related. When I asked, he didn't hesitate at all to say yes. I was so excited to have someone I felt comfortable with taking on the job. I don't think I ever got a chance to tell him to thank you. A couple of years ago, his passing shocked our entire graduating class. I will cherish the fond memories I had that day with Edward…Sleep in peace, my friend. My junior prom was coming up, and I had planned to wear the dress from the pageant to the event. That week, Granny had planned to be a chaperone with my sister Ayana to the D.C. Zoo so that she would be gone Friday. I took it upon myself to do something to "facilitate" everything I needed to do to prepare for the prom that night since she would not be back from the trip until later. At the time, I dabbled a lot with other creative skills, such as hair styling and doing nails.

My girlfriend, Sontrice Graham asked if I would do her nails for the prom. Sontrice and I had known each other since the 6th grade. Her Mom was a hairstylist and Granny's been her client for a few years. So on Wednesday, we set it up that I would come over after school that Friday to do her nails so they would be fresh for the prom. I also had my plan in mind, and I had seen other kids get away with all the time…I was going to cut school. The plan was to leave school, go to the salon and do everything I needed for the prom before Granny got home from the trip. So that Thursday, I had forged Granny's signature, and wrote a letter saying that I had permission to leave school at noon Friday. I had been practicing her signature all week to make it look believable. I turned the note in to the attendance office as soon as I got to school Friday morning. They would then have to call the house, but I knew Granny wouldn't be there, so the letter would show proof of parental permission. When I didn't get an early dismissal slip, I felt something was wrong. I tried not to think about it though. All I could think about was getting to the prom with my crush.

I had a crush on this boy for so long. But instead, we became good friends. I became like a counselor to him when it came to girls. He even asked me to hook him up or say a few words on his behalf to some of my friends. I did, but I always wondered, "What is it about them that I don't have?" I was even more excited when I asked him to the junior prom. He was so cute and muscular for his age. That boy was FINE. Man, oh, man. His name was Kyrie Clarkson. He was on the football team and was pretty popular around school. We had planned to be chauffeured by his Mom's boyfriend in a Jaguar, so the thought of arriving in style was so cool. We had everything planned to a tee. After school, I went to Sontrice's, as planned, and did her nails. I kept looking at the time because I still had to get myself ready, curl my hair, freshen up, and get dressed before Kyrie came to the house. When Granny picked me up, I could feel a bit of tension in the air, but I didn't mention it.

As soon as we got home, I ran into the house to start my bath water and turned on the curlers sitting on my dresser. I wanted to make sure they would be good and hot when I got out of the tub. As I was soaking, Granny was in her bedroom with the door open. I had the bathroom door closed but I heard her talking. I cracked it a bit so I could hear what she was saying. "Shawaun, where are you going?" she asked.

"I'm going to the prom Granny, remember? Kyrie and his Mom should be here in about an hour to pick me up."

"I don't know what you were thinking, but you're not going anywhere." My heart STOPPED. "WHAT? This can't be?" I thought.

"Granny, what do you mean? Kyrie and his Mom are on the way to get me." I explained.

"Well, you're gonna have to tell him you're not going. You ain't going nowhere." Man, you could've bought me for a penny at that moment. I'm wondering where all this was coming from. I'm pleading my case at this point, and Granny wasn't budging.

"You better tell that boy you ain't going when he gets here." she said.

"I can't tell him that. That's too embarrassing, Granny. His Mom is going to be here too…I can't do that."

"Okay then, I WILL." And she did just that.

When Kyrie and his Mom pulled up, I was in my room with the door cracked so that I could listen to what was said. My Granny wasn't playing. She went down there and told Kyrie and his Mom to their faces that I was **not** going and that they needed to leave. At that moment, I wish I could've just shriveled up and died. "This shit is gonna be the talk around the school on Monday." Granny came back upstairs, opened my door, and said, "Next time you decide to sign my name for something, I suggest you ask first." *DAMN.*

I had forgotten about the letter I took to the attendance office. Come to find out, they did call my house, but Granny hadn't left yet. She had been holding that information all day. Monday at school, I was the TALK of the junior class.

Kyrie had told EVERYONE what had happened. Hell, I would've too if the shoe was on the other foot. People were coming up to me all day about the prom and what they would've done in my situation. That was all fine and good, but they didn't have a grandmother like me. Granny didn't play, and she MEANT business.

SENIOR YEAR... I couldn't believe my public school education was almost over. It's crazy to think that all the kids I'd practically grown up with will be moving on with their lives as we all graduate. Some of them I may never see or be in contact with again. It was kinda sad to think about, but it was a good thing at the same time. It makes you realize how precious time is and how it is essential to build relationships while you have access to them. I was still up in the air about college, but I decided to apply to Virginia State University. If that didn't come through, I would just go to community college and transfer after acquiring an associates degree. This year graduation fell on my birthday, so it would be even more memorable for me. I was turning 18 and it still hurt knowing that my Mom couldn't celebrate it with me the way I'd like to. I dreamed of her all the time.

One time I dream that I could smell someone cooking liver and onions in the kitchen, which was one of her favorite dishes. She would have so many onions in pan that the steam throughout the house would damn near burned out your retina. I would be crying for no reason. In the dream I could smell the aroma, and immediately got out of bed headed downstairs. Granny hadn't cooked that meal in forever. My siblings didn't like it, and I had stopped eating that dish after my Mom's accident.

When I got to the opening of the kitchen, I saw what looked like my Mom. She had her back turned facing towards the sink. "Cheryl?" I said. She turned around, and I could feel the tears welled up, as they streamed down my face like a flood. The joyful emotion I felt at that moment, knowing she was okay. "You're Here." I said and gave her the biggest hug.

And then I woke up. I sat up in my bed thinking, "Oh my God, that was too real." It didn't feel like a dream, as I wiped away the wetness on my face. Dream on, dreamer, your dream WILL come true. I thought to myself. I needed that dream to come true quick, fast and in a hurry.

My Granddaddy had fallen ill in the last few months. We had to convert his room basically to a hospital room. He was bedridden pretty much, but could walk with assistance if needed. I remember one time Granny had put him in the bathtub so that he could wash up. He was trying to get out and fell on the floor. I had to pick him up to get him to his room. I truly understand now what "dead weight" really means. He was very small due to the declining weight loss, but felt like he weighed a ton. By May of 1994, the doctors said there was nothing else they could do for Granddaddy, and to keep him comfortable until his demise. So we began to prepare for the inevitable. I thought about how the two of them had such a rough marriage, yet Granny still cared for him.

Remember the movie Diary of a Mad Black Woman by Tyler Perry? THAT was Granny. For all the years he treated her badly, she made him understand the hell he put her through. She continued to cook for him, bathe him, and monitored him even in his decline. To her, it was like taking care of a patient because they hadn't slept in the same room for over 10 years. It was troubling seeing my Granddaddy that way. When I would go into his room, he would say, "Look at all those cows outside." We lived on a residential street with no farmland in sight. I knew then it wouldn't be long before we would be saying goodbye.

A few days later, the phone rang during the wee hours of the morning. It wasn't even time for me to get up yet for school. I heard Granny answer the phone and say "Hello," and nothing else was said. I heard her hang up the phone; then I heard movement. She came to my room and said, "I have some bad news; Eva and George were killed in a car crash on the highway coming from the country", and she went back to her room.

This was my Great Aunt Eva and her husband, George. She was younger than my Granny, but she was like the "glue" of the family. She was so lively and such a fashionista. She could dress her tail off and made sure her granddaughters did too. I began to reminisce about when she came to our house or when we visited her home in the Highland Park area. Man, I'll never forget the last basement party Granny had when I was a little kid. Aunt Eva and Uncle George were drunk as hell, but they turned the party out that night. They were down there doing "the dog," which was a dance that had come out to go along with the song made by George Clinton called "Atomic Dog". I took pictures that night, and we laughed for days after. Damn, I'm surely going to miss them.

I know EVERYONE in our family is missing a piece of their heart right now. Believe it or not, they died on my Granddaddy's REAL birthday. For over 40years, my Granddaddy thought his birthday was on May 22, when really it was May 21, and he never knew…go figure.

The funeral arrangements were set for a week out; and since it was close to my graduation, Aunt Janice decided to come down and stay until then. It was indeed a somber moment for our family. One thing about Granny though, she never shed a tear. She was a pillar of strength, solid as a rock even. The Bible says that "the rocks will cry out", I guess that never meant Granny. She's like the Rock of Gibraltar, and I'd **never** seen her break.

CHAPTER 8

MY LIFE

We were gearing up for Graduation FINALLY. That week, Granny took me shopping to get my graduation outfit. It was becoming real to me at this point that I was about to go to college. I had gotten accepted to Virginia State, which surprised me a bit. My SAT scores weren't the best, but I was able to get by. We were all excited about our futures at school and saddened that we wouldn't see each other anymore. We all grew up together, and now we're separating. But that's life for you. Due to the loss of my Great Aunt and Uncle a few weeks ago, it was good to have a bit of a distraction from the tragedy of the loss. I did get to the prom this year. I guess I should've been excited, but it turned out to be a nightmare. I had designed my dress for the dance, and Ms. Deborah from years ago made it for me. Well, the dress didn't come out the way I envisioned it. I'm one of those people who can see a complete look in my head; then do my best to execute it.

I scheduled to get my hair done by my regular stylist. I gave him a picture and explained my idea to him. I entrusted that he would have me looking fabulous as he always does, but to my dismay, THAT was not the case. Instead of tapering my hair in the back, he shaved it off. I felt like a "Bald-head scallywag" coming out of the salon. Then I went to get my nails done at the nail school by my house. I had gone there numerous times before, and they always did a great job. Not this time. My nails were all lumpy and bumpy and weren't even shaped correctly. So here I am, dress messed up, hair bald, with amateur looking nails…I was PISSED. If it had been cold, you would've seen the STEAM coming from my ears.

Luckily, I had a date with another guy with whom I had a semi-crush on during my senior year. His name was Samson Lenard, and he was pretty cool. Again, he was known in his own right, so it was good knowing that I would be on the arm of someone pretty known throughout our class. I had a circle of friends, but I was on lockdown most of the time from Granny, so I didn't have much of a social life outside of school. So I had told them that I was wearing a gold dress, and he said that we would be double dating his homeboy, Lorenz and his date, LaTeshia. I was excited to have some redemption from last year. But I was beginning to feel that it would be short-lived with all that was happening. Since I was turning 18 in a few weeks, Granny said, "Well, you're about to be grown, so that you can stay out late after the prom." "For real, Granny?" I said. And she gave me a nod of acceptance. I felt like the ball and chain had finally come off. I felt free and ready to get out and enjoy myself for once.

I was ready to go and waiting on my date. They were already late, so I was getting a bit antsy. When they arrived, I saw Sammy coming toward the house, and I turned to grab my purse. When I turned back around, I looked at him with a bit of disgust. "Damn, could ANYTHING else go wrong." I thought. I specifically told this boy I was wearing a gold dress. Why did he show up with a burgundy and black paisley tie and cummerbund? On top of that, he and his homeboy matched with the other girl LeTeisha, who had on a black dress. "What the Hell. It's only the biggest night of my high school career." I can't look back now, it is what it is. We got to the venue, and we were all excited about taking our pictures and just having a good time. This was probably the last formal event we would spend together, making it even more special.

The night seemed to go on forever. The music was blasting in the hotel ballroom, and the crowd was lit. Looking around at all the girls sparkling in the light, and the guys looking dapper, showed that we ALL cleaned up pretty well. It was time for the final song, and the DJ went out with a bang. He played "Anything" by SWV. As soon as the song began, the crowd grew with excitement. "THIS IS IT. IT'S FINISHED".

When leaving the prom, it was kind of late. We didn't meet up early enough to eat before, so we had to get some food from whatever was still open, so Taco Bell it was. We each got a little something to eat, and now I'm even more excited about what's next. I overheard some people talking at the prom about an afterparty at the LaQuinta Inn, and since Granny gave me the "green light," I was ready. "So, are we headed to the afterparty after this?" I asked. "Well, WE are. We are taking you home. Your grandmother is not going to cuss us out." Lorenz said. I couldn't BELIEVE this. I FINALLY get to stay out, and now I'm STILL going home early? All because of some shit LAST year? "Uggghhh". So to the house I went, ending my night as I always did; doing nothing.

The BIG day is finally here. I've been anticipating this moment since elementary school. On the way to the Mosque where the Graduation was being held, all I could think was NO MORE PUBLIC SCHOOL. No more having to get up early to catch the bus or after-school activities. No pep rallies or school trips, and no teachers calling you to come back to class in the hall. It was over. Today was even more unique because it was my 18th birthday, one I will never forget. Walking in, I began taking pictures of every one of my classmates. I knew that we were all going in different directions, so I wanted to capture the memories. The day was going just as we had practiced, and then it was time for the processional. The anticipation of walking out there as soon-to-be graduates was overwhelming. We each sat in our respective seats upon hearing our names being called. I can't remember who spoke the final speech, but I do remember that Samantha Crews was our Valedictorian. She wanted to be a doctor and was headed to Howard University. She became a Pediatrician and Head of the Pediatric Dept. of a major hospital. Dreams do come true for some people.

As the speaker finished the speech, I thought, "What will happen now? Would I make it at VSU? Am I ready for this?" We all stood row by row as we were called to collect our diplomas. When they got to my name, all my school years flashed before my eyes.

I looked in the crowd and saw my Aunt, Granny, and siblings waving. I was glad they were there to support me, but I wish my Mom had been there. I know she would've been so proud to see me walk across the stage. Oh well, some dreams are just that, fragments of our imagination.

That night was Granny's bingo night, so Aunt Janice and I decided to go with her. I remember always going with Granny when I was little. I loved it. Being around all the old folks being loud and smoking their cigarettes made me feel grown up too. But the best part for me was the concession stand. They had the best fries. We were all playing our cards, looking to win something. I got close to winning a few games, with one or two numbers left to be called. Then it was time for the final game of the evening, the Jackpot coverall. You had to stamp all of the numbers called, and whichever card had all the numbers covered, was the winner. The tension was getting thick up in there. One lady had called out "Bingo," but it turned out to be a false alarm because she stamped a number that wasn't called. I had two left on my card, and so did Granny. "B 15," the caller said. That was one of my numbers.

Now I had one left; I had G 50 for the win. This game paid out $1000, so I was already anticipating how I would spend it. As the following number was about to be called, I held my breath and said a silent prayer, "God, let it be me." "G 50." OMG. I won. I said to myself. I gave Granny my paper so she could call bingo for me. "B-I-N-G-O," she yelled out loud and proud. To my dismay, another person yelled out as well, so the attendants had to verify that each call was a valid winner. My card was valid, but so was the other person. I didn't get the whole prize but walking away with half felt damn good. I gave Granny $100 and my Aunt $100, and I kept the rest. It came on time too because I needed to pay $150 for my dorm fee, so God was looking out. I began to understand that God had His hand in every area of my life, even when I was unaware.

Heading to college was a significant deal. When I helped my Big Sis, Angenette, I thought about moving into her dorm when I was little. I thought my experience would be similar. Ahh…NO. It wasn't. I had nothing to take to my dorm room, so I applied and qualified for a JC Penny store card. I got everything I wanted for my dorm room. A comforter, sheets, pillows, a rug, and a few other things. What made it even better was that my Mom was being transferred to a Nursing facility not far from the school. The nursing home where she was over Church Hill tried to kill her by giving her an overdose of downers, so we moved her. The next place was in a "white" neighborhood that treated her well. But my Mom was very disrespectful at times, which prompted them to terminate her stay. I was just glad that now I could keep an eye on her more since she was closer.

On move in day, I met my roommate from the Brooklyn's Crown Heights area. Her name was Kim, and she was SUPER tall. Her parents were very nice, and they invited me to go to dinner with all of them since my people had left. They were kind, trying to get to know me, and I was trying not to have them get to know me too much. Now that I was older, it was easy to cover things and mask my flaws. The apple doesn't fall too far from the tree. Over the next few weeks, I introduced her to some people I had met during the orientation, and sometimes we would all hang out together. But she and I didn't click. She was friendly, but we didn't mesh, no matter how hard we tried. She was bold and boisterous, whereas I had become meek, mild, and passive.

Honestly, I began to go through a major depression. I was going to class, and although some of my classes seemed hard, I still gave my best effort. English was my favorite subject in school. I've loved English and Language Arts throughout my high school career. I had some great teachers by the way. They all added a bit of spark to my writing and my perception of writing. One of my teachers, Mrs. Moeser, always commented on my handwriting. She would always say, "Shawaun, you have such lovely penmanship." I would always smile and think of Baby Joe, and how it was because of him I did. He always made me practice when I would mention his handwriting and how beautiful it was.

I wanted to put that same energy into my college-level English class as well. I remember when the grades came out near the end of the quarter, my professor gave me an F. I should've questioned her about it or found out how she came up with that grade. Instead of challenging her, I took that as a direct hit personally. With that, I began to look at myself as everyone in my family had told me so many times before. I'm STUPID. I wore that "F" like a scarlet letter for a very long time. I began to question and second guess my reasons for even being in school in the first place. That one moment changed the course of my college experience. From then on, I would get up like usual, take my shower, and prepare for class. At the time, my roommate Kim had an earlier class than I did.

I would be getting dressed as she was leaving for class. As soon as she would leave, I would get back in my bed, put the covers over my head, and stay there and cry until it was time for her to come back. I began doing this every day. I felt like the weight of the world was on my shoulders. Here I was, the first in my family to go to college, and I was flunking out.

Then, my Mom was like 20 minutes away from the school driving, but I still couldn't get to see her because it was too far for me to walk. Then I was reaching out to my Dad to try to rekindle or start a relationship, but every time I needed something, he couldn't help or still seemed unavailable. I was crumbling at the seams, yet no one knew because I masked it so well. Man, if you really looked at my life, then you would see what I saw, wallowing in a pit of despair.

I began hanging out with the girl next door to my room. Her name was Sherica Smith, from Baltimore, Maryland. She discovered that I could fix hair well and asked that I do hers. She loved her hair so much that she REFUSED to tell people that I did it so that I wouldn't get any more customers. She would always say, "Girl, I can't let nobody know you do my hair. I can't have other people copying my style." She was too funny. She reminded me of a pit bull in a skirt, and not that she was ugly. She had a straightforward attitude but was very stylish. She was the only girl on our floor with a room to herself, and we hit it off immediately. We found that we had so much in common.

I was over there so much that I just moved on in. It was as if I was drawn to her spirit and needed to be around her light. I was operating in my phase of darkness every day, so being around her made me shift that energy at times. Our childhoods both represented periods of struggle, but the difference was that she prayed every day. She spoke of her "praying" Grandmother all the time. It was funny because she affectionately called her "Granny" like I did MY Granny.

I had the opportunity to meet her grandmother as well. Mrs. Cheek was a remarkable woman. She was such a joy, but she didn't take any shit off anybody. And Sherica got her taste in style because her Granny STAYED fly. When Sherica planned to go home for the weekend, she invited me to come with her. I had never visited Baltimore before, although my Great Aunt Rose lived there. She was one of my Granny's sisters as well. We stayed the weekend in her childhood home, where she lived with her Granny. Both her and my Granny were dark brown with beautifully smooth skin. Both were small and short, but their aura and spirit made them 10x their size. Mrs. Cheek reminded me a lot of Granny. I was able to meet most of her family too. And she showed me all the spots that she grew up around like I was getting an intimate tour of her world as she knew it.

I met her, Auntie, Uncle, and a slew of cousins. They made me feel like I was a part of their family. Her mom's sister was a Pastor, and the church was an accredited school as well. Mostly all her kids and grandchildren were very actively involved in the day-to-day functioning. I remember it was bigger than any church I had been to. My family didn't go to church regularly like that. My Granny was a holiday goer. She attended on Palm Sunday, Easter, Thanksgiving, and Christmas, but that was it. She did make me go some Sundays with our neighbors across the street, Mr. & Mrs. Bowen. They were an elderly couple, old enough to be Granny's parents almost. That weekend, she took me to Sunday Service with her family. I was a bit nervous and didn't know what to expect.

When we walked in, people were everywhere. Sunday school was wrapping up, so many classrooms were filled with adults and children. Everyone was dressed in their Sunday best. Looking back, it showed how many will dress up outwardly to cover the hidden broken pieces they inwardly hold onto. I sensed that many people I was looking at fit that mold. We were ALL walking around somewhat like we "had it all together", when we were projecting who we wanted to be and not understanding our true birthright. The Bible says, "All things that the Father hath are mine". So, we are each divinely given dominion and authority to have whatever we speak or desire. Many of us walk blindfolded in life; Shoot, I know I did for a long time. But being here made me see how many of us were going through the "same" motions. We were existing and NOT genuinely living.

As the service was getting ready to start, we found seating up front on the right-hand side of the church. Sherica, Mrs. Cheek, her Mom, and I all sat in the same row. I was intrigued by how the service was going. She was part of a non-denominational church, but they functioned or operated like the Church of God in Christ.

Those that are from the church world would understand. As the music started, people began shouting, clapping, and rejoicing. Suddenly, a lady two rows behind began to shout so hard and loud that she "caught" the Holy Ghost and started dancing everywhere. Then another lady ran out of the aisle and ran around the church, hollering, "Thank you, God. Thank you, God". Again, this was all new to me.

I was literally standing there as if I were a spectator at a concert, looking at the performances around me. It was like a chain reaction after that. People everywhere were getting the Holy Spirit. I began to look around, and I saw Sherica, her Mom, and Granny were getting it IN. "Is it gonna hit me too?" I began to think to myself. Then I began to feel neglected because everyone else was flowing in the spirit around me, and I wished I could experience the feeling as well. I didn't "get the spirit" that day, but later in life, I understood its symbolism and was able to operate on that level because it is indeed a gift. After the service, I did feel a bit lighter though. I may not have danced around, but the joy was felt. We then left to have dinner with her Aunt and the whole crew. It felt good to see all of her family together that way, which was something I hadn't experienced in a long time with my family.

They were all laughing, joking, and having a good time. Her Aunt Sharon's house was beautiful, like a mansion to me. It was so spacious. I also had the opportunity to meet her Dad. That man was so funny. He was a natural-born comedian. He was tall, with a bald head, a pot belly, and a husky voice. He would say "In B-more, you better watch what you say and where; it may be life or death for you if you don't". He was fun-loving and ruthless at the same time. I remember how he surprised Sherica with a car to drive back to school. "I got a surprise for you," he said and handed her a box that looked like it was made for jewelry.

"Oh, you got me a necklace?" she said. "Just open the damn box." When she opened the box, she started slowly, anticipating some bling. To her surprise, it was some old keys. "What's this?" Sherica said, "It's your surprise; I got you a car." "THESE old things. Ugghh." Omg, I cracked up. The expression on her face was priceless. She was expecting something a lot newer than what she got. When we went to look at the car in the back, I'm telling you, the look on her face is one I'll never forget. I damn near peed on myself laughing so hard.

That wouldn't be the last time we've had some crazy moments. We were both comedy movie buffs. And that year, Martin Lawrence came out with a new stand up called "You So Crazy." Oh my God, we laughed so hard over that movie that BOTH of us would be in tears or have our stomachs cramping. We would watch it over and over when we needed a good laugh. One time Sherica was laughing so hard that she was in a fetal position on the floor. Our RA came by doing her rounds on our floor and believed she was in distress. She knocked at the door and saw her on the floor. "She's fine, Dawn; she's just laughing," I said. She had the most dazed and confused look, but she slowly walked away. Or the time she set me up on a blind date. I was so mad at her that day. That shit was funny as hell now that I think about it. She was dating this guy on campus named Levon. I believe he played football for VSU, and they were going to the campus hangout on a date. She didn't want to go by herself, so I guess she asked if he had a friend for me so I could go too, which he did.

"Shawaun, come with me and Levon to The Pit tonight, I don't wanna go by myself."

"I'm not trying to be no third wheel, Rica." I said.

"Naw, girl, he got a friend for you. So it will be like a double date." she said.

"Hmmmm, I don't know. I got a bad feeling about this. I don't do blind dates."

"C'mon, Girl. It's gonna be fine." The more she insisted, the more my spidey sense was saying, "HELL NO SHAWAUN.... DON'T DO IT." But this was my ace boon, so I gave in and decided to go. Let me just say my intuition DON'T lie. We both got dressed to go downstairs and were walking out of Howard Hall, where we stayed. Levon had his back turned, facing his friend, so I couldn't see him. "Lord, PLEASE don't let this boy be ugly", I kept saying to myself.

As we walked out, she says, "Hey, Levon." He turns around with a smile, and I look behind him to see this gorilla looking gooney goo goo behind him. I told Sherica I didn't have a good feeling about this, and THIS was why I don't do blind dates. This proved my point. Oh my gosh, I wanted to just turn around and walk the fuck off. She saw the look on my face and tried to divert the energy by introducing us.

"This is my girl Shawaun, and you are?"

"Oh, my name is John, What up?" he said.

"Ain't nothing up nigga," I thought, but I replied with "Hi, nice to meet you." Well, I didn't hold up to my end of the deal. As we were walking across the field towards the campus restaurant called "The Pit", I turned and left her with our famous line from the movie, "I gotta go, see you when I see you."

Sherica and I were close to two other girls on our floor named Tasha and Taylor, who were roommates also. So we considered ourselves a "clique". The "S" & "T" girls. It was corny come to think of it, but it was all in fun. The funny part was Sherica and I were virgins at the time, so we knew nothing about sexual intercourse. Tasha and Taylor though, knew all too well. The two of them would give us pointers because they were no amateurs in the game. We would all be in our room, and they would school us on just about anything sex-related. I became friends with another girl on my floor from Louisa County, and her name was Chondra Koffey. Along with her roommate, she and I hung out a few times. Chondra was the only freshman at the time; I knew that she had a car on campus. She would go back home every weekend to see her boyfriend back home.

As the girls and I got closer, my depression grew more robust, and then I added alcohol. I wasn't old enough to buy it, but Tasha knew someone who would get it for us. That became an every weekend routine, and I would drink my problems away. We were getting ready for the homecoming event that year, and I was excited. I remember the artist "Miss Jones" was performing. She's now a top radio personality on Hot 97 in New York. It was cool to see an artist with my last name, so I was looking forward to it. Tasha told me that her friend would get the drinks for us to have some before going to the gym for the concert.

We met up in a wooded area on campus, and she showed me the spread of options. We had Mad Dog 20/20, Boones farm, and beer. I never really liked beer, and I saw my family drink that. Each sip turned to a gulp as I was trying my best to slip into another zone where nothing and no one was a hindrance to me. So the fruit drinks were a better option for me. I realized that alcohol gave me the courage to speak loudly and make my voice heard. I was so drunk walking across campus to the gym. Honestly, I don't remember much that night. I remember walking into the gym and seeing people standing around dancing. It was as if my vision had blurred, so I couldn't see ANYTHING or anyone clearly if they weren't right in front of me.

However, I DO remember trying my best to get to the bathroom without wetting my pants. It seemed like the longest walk up those stairs, but I did make it. Soon the declining grades, missed classes, and morbid thoughts became too much to bear. I stayed one more year there and left VSU in December of 1995. I couldn't deal with the stigma of being on academic probation and the perception of other people's opinions, so I left. It's crazy how that one grade freshman year affected my self-esteem that much. I was torn emotionally, and I began to crack little by little. If only people REALLY looked into my life.

CHAPTER 9

BE HAPPY

I was back home with Granny, trying to pick up the pieces of my life and earn some money. Since the school route didn't work, I had to do something to keep me busy. One of the girls I befriended in college left, and we began to hang out more often. Chondra had done well for herself since we last talked. She was doing customer service in the warranty department of a major retailer and was one of their top sellers. She managed to create a lucrative lifestyle for herself and rented a home of her own. Being 20 and 21 years of age and doing THAT well was commendable. She and I would go out to clubs a lot, and she always asked me to do her hair. During our times together, I was able to meet most of her family. She had a similar story as well, but she was raised in the country. One thing about her though, was that she drew a lot of attention because she had an athletic yet feminine shape, she had developed from being a cheerleader. Going out with her was always an adventure.

I was having fun, but I needed to find something permanent to occupy my time. My siblings were still young and were having some issues behaviorally in school. I know a lot of it had to do with the fact that they really had no one to talk to about how they were feeling or what had happened to our Mom. I began spending more time at their school, which was my alma mater. I would go every day and spend time with my sister's class and be an extra help to her teacher.

Then another teacher, who taught my brother in 1st-grade, took me under her wing. Mrs. Quinn was old school when it came to teaching. She had a system that was undeniably accurate.

She had created a proven process of mastering the education machine. I call it "the machine" because she had organized a routine where daily the children had specific activities to enhance their level of reading and comprehension, while learning to speak phonetically properly.

She was a beast at what she did and taught me how to do the same. I would go every day to the school to work with her. We had developed a bond outside of school as well. At times, I would go with her after school to her house, where I was able to meet Mr. Quinn.

The two of them were so cute to me. She was very boisterous and direct, yet he was very calm and wise in a sense. He was also very humorous and always cracked side jokes about things Mrs. Quinn was saying. I would laugh so hard at the two of them. She never realized that they both gave me a positive image of marriage. They had two adult children who had both gone to college and excelled. One was a Medical Doctor, while the other was a Physicist. I could sense feelings of pride as they spoke of their children and the life they built for them. Mr. Quinn was a former military man, who was very hard-working, yet had no formal education. He was self-taught in many areas but very articulate and sound in his decision-making. Mrs. Quinn was college educated and focused on being a model for her children, which they followed. She was not only a creator in the classroom, but she and Mr. Quinn had shown how they created harmony within their marriage. I began looking at them as parental figures. She picked me up every day at 5 am in the summer, and we walked the track.

We would walk for about an hour and a half, or roughly 3-4 miles daily. We were doing this 7 days a week. I lost over 20 lbs. that summer and was looking good. I felt better about myself, and confidence was oozing from my pores. Granny didn't really like the fact that I was spending so much time with Mrs. Quinn and looked down on her somewhat.

"I see you still hanging around Mrs. Quinn? Keep on. She's gonna hurt your feelings soon enough." she would say. I never believed that to be true. Now granted, Mrs. Quinn was very nosey but meant no harm by it. And because I had learned her in such a way, I knew what and what not to discuss around her, just in case.

I wanted to get my driver's license, but Granny wouldn't let me use her car. After Mrs. Quinn saw my dilemma, she and Mr. Quinn decided that I would drive one of their cars to take the driving test. I was so excited and humbled that they would do such a thing for me. I couldn't wait to get to the DMV the next day, so I could get this done. She came to pick me up, and we headed to the motor vehicle office. I left there that day as a licensed Virginia driver. She was proud of me, but I was prouder of myself. From then on, I noticed how God always had "a ram in the bush" for me. She would be one of the many people along the way to add value and substance to my life. Now with a driver's license, it opened up so many doors. I still didn't have a car, but it gave me more hope that I would have one soon. Well, back to square one. Got to do something. So, I decided to enroll in the local community college.

I even began attending church and joined the choir there. The day I decided to surrender my life to Christ, I was so overwhelmed with emotion. The song the choir was singing was "Be Encouraged" by William Becton. I remember walking down the aisle and feeling the weight of the world dissipating from my shoulders. I felt light as if I had released years of pain by making that decision. When the service was over, I was approached by a young man who was interning at the church. His name was Corey Willis, and he offered to give me a ride home since he knew I rode the church van there. I was at the service with my younger sister, so he gave us both a ride back to the house. He was a student at Virginia Union University at the time and was a father to a small son. He was very nice and handsome, and I thought he was really sweet. He and I both had joined the church that day, which was cool. We exchanged numbers when he brought me home, and we began spending a lot of our time together.

He had his own apartment with his roommate Darius, and I went over to his crib to hang out. He was not my first sexual experience. The first had been a few months ago with a guy from high school. He and I were really good friends, and one day when I knew no one would be home, I invited him over. Kalick was 6 '3" with a dark chocolate brown complexion. I was smitten with him, but we never really crossed those lines until that day. We were in my Granny's basement on the sofa. I had just come from out of the shower when he arrived and had my towel wrapped around me. I straddled him as I advanced myself upon him. All I could think about was everything that my Mom had told me in that last conversation about sex. As he entered me, I thought I was gonna DIE. He was so large. Too large for a beginner. It didn't last long, a few strokes at best due to the pain. When I rose, I saw that my hymen had broken, and there were small amounts of blood. In my mind, it hurt like hell, but I was no longer a virgin. I went to the school later with Mrs. Quinn, grinning from ear to ear.

With Corey, it was different. Being intimate with him felt like the best thing since sliced bread. Yet, according to my doctor, he was just drilling a new one, if you know what I mean. Too much friction caused major irritation for me. Then I noticed that I became very insecure. I remember he let me use his car one day, and I told him I was going to my Granny's. I ended up going to Mr. and Mrs. Quinn's house for a while and to the store, so I never made it to Granny's. When I got back to the church, he said, "I thought you were going to your Granny's? Where were you?"

"I did go to her house." I said.

"No, you didn't because I called her to see if you had got there yet." The look on my face spoke a thousand words. Instead of me just telling him the truth, I lied. Why? I don't know, but that marked a turning point for the worst. He kept asking, and I kept deflecting, I stormed out of the church and began walking aimlessly. I walked for what seemed like moments, but really it was 2 1/2 hours total. I remember having on some blue jean overalls and a red leather coat. It was cold, and a bit of snow blanketed the ground.

I had a moment where it felt like the devil on my left shoulder and God on my right. I was having a battle in my mind about my life and everything to that point. "Why did I lie like that? I should have told him the truth." I began to speak all the negative self-talk that I'd heard directed to me for years. I even thought it would be best if I just took my life, then I wouldn't have to worry about it anymore. I was walking past a pile of leaves on the ground, and the negative entity said, "Just bury yourself in those leaves and be done with it." Then the other side said, "No, Shawaun. You gotta keep going, don't give up." I kept walking and passed the mental hospital called Westbrook. I looked at it and the negative entity began talking again. "Go admit yourself. You're crazy, remember? Nobody can help you. You need to be put away." Again, I wrestled with the thought. I was always told I was crazy and felt even more so now that my mind was in a tug of war with my subconscious. "You flunked out of school because you weren't good enough. I don't know why you even tried. Such a waste of time, do everybody a favor and get rid of yourself." The messages were coming stronger and stronger like radio frequency waves to my ears. It was so cold, and I was so tired, but something in me said, "keep walking," so I did. I got to the end of the block, and it was by the main road. I saw a huge tractor-trailer coming, and this time I heard, "Walk out into the road and let it hit you. Then all this will be over. No more worries for you."

As I began to walk towards the curb, to walk out into the road to my demise, I heard yet another voice; this one was calm but direct. "This is NOT the end, Shawaun. This is NOT YOUR TIME. Keep walking. I'm preparing you, but you must keep going. Life doesn't end because things didn't go as you planned or things didn't work out as you hoped. It's going to get better. Trust me. This is only temporary." It was as if the glare from the truck woke me up, and I immediately jumped back on the sidewalk before the truck was within inches of hitting me. I then began to talk to myself. I began to encourage myself, "Shawaun, you GOT this.

You can't stop now. Life has been hard, but you can make it. You're NOT a failure. You are smart. It's just that the world doesn't want to recognize it yet. I know you're tired, but keep going, keep moving." I continued to walk and coached myself all the way to his house, a total of about 10 miles. When I got to his apartment, I fell out on the bed and crashed. My body was physically tired, and my mind was mentally whipped. I had just won the first battle for my life.

Things were beginning to look up, though. Mrs. Quinn was able to connect me with a job as a Preschool Instructional Assistant with Richmond Public Schools. This was my first real job as an adult. The summer before, I had gone to Massachusetts with my Aunt Janice, where I worked two jobs. That summer, she had her daughter, which she had predicted after my graduation. "Shawaun, I'm going to California, and I'm coming back pregnant." And believe it or not, she did just that. Even then, that showed me the power we have in our words and to be mindful of what we put into the atmosphere. Working at the school was great for me, but my time management sucked. I was late just about every day. In my mind, it didn't matter if I was late, but that I showed up at all. The teacher I was working under did not see things from my point of view. I remember the first week before the start of school, we prepared the setup of the room for the children.

This was right up my alley because I was doing this with Mrs. Quinn for free, and now I'm being paid to do it. The teacher I worked under was named Ms. Arcasian, and she was fresh out of college. She seemed nice, but she turned out to be very jealous of me and my role in "her " classroom. On the first day of school, she would have the kids come in and play in a designated area while she would talk to the parents about the curriculum. Unfortunately, the plan changed at the last minute, and she wanted ME to talk to the parents while she worked with the children. Things went very smoothly, but to her surprise, the parents ended up coming to me about EVERYTHING. I explained to them in all honesty, "she" was the actual teacher, and I was her aide. They did not like that at all since they had already established communication with me.

My relationship with Corey continued to progress, although I felt extremely guilty for lying to him for no reason. The coursework at school was becoming somewhat of a bore to me, and I found myself drifting away. I guess the fear that I had built up about being a failure was starting to stick with me. I felt like this may not be a good avenue for me due to the outcome at VSU. I had linked up again with Chondra, and we would hang out on the weekends clubbing. I had met a few guys there but was reluctant to jump into anything. I talked to them from time to time, but nothing official. Corey and I were becoming quite rocky, which is why I felt I should explore other options.

One of the guys I met at the club began pursuing me more, named Lenny. He would call and check up on me and was very attentive to my needs and concerns. It was like a breath of fresh air for me. He seemed so nice and unlike others who had approached me before. He was the beginning of the pattern in a lot of ways. He was super smart and charismatic, and he hustled on the side, which showed great "potential" in my mind. I've come to realize that potential can only take you so far. Without action, it's just bullshit wrapped up in a beautiful gift box with nothing in it. We began talking just about every day. He didn't have a car, but he and his cousin would come to pick me up in the mornings so that I would get to work on time. I thought that was so sweet of him. Even without a vehicle, he was looking out for my best interest. I was growing to like him a lot.

About 6 months had gone by, and he was still coming at me. Corey and I had fizzled out and were in an on-again-off-again cycle. I had planned on going to this party with Chondra that Corey invited me to. So she and I went together and were ready to turn up. What I failed to mention is that Richmond is really small. Although it is the capital, it's as if the communities were intertwined, and everybody KNOWS everybody. So when I got to the party, I saw Corey with his friends standing close to the DJ. As I was walking towards him, and got a tap on my arm. I look around and it's Lenny.

In my mind, I was thinking, "Oh shit. They are BOTH here." But being the chameleon that I had trained myself to be, I played it cool and discreet. Unfortunately, Corey watched me talk to this guy, and a big argument ensued in the parking lot. Corey's older brother was trying to keep him calm. "You better bring your ass to my crib tonight so we can talk." I then told Lenny that I would have to talk to him later. I began to feel really bad, and felt like all this was my fault. Now to some degree, it also showed me that doors must be fully closed when moving forward. You can't leave a door cracked and not expect something or someone to come through. So for me, the growing bond with Lenny had to end. Corey would have to be my main focus. I went back to his place that night, and we had "make-up" sex. It was good, but deep inside, my heart was no longer in it as it was before.

At the school, we had planned a field trip to the circus and were collecting money for the trip. I remember a parent was asking for a bit of an extension since she hadn't received her pay yet. I then did what I would've done for anyone. I offered to pay for the child to attend and have her pay me back later that week. By the time it was all said and done, I had paid for 3 of my students to go. Ms. Arcasian had gotten wind of what I did and reported me to the principal. She began to do this at least once a week until I was ultimately fired. I always wondered why she felt threatened by me. It wasn't my fault that the parents talked to me before her. That's what she implemented from Day 1. She had me speaking with the parents while operating in my role as an aide with the children. It made me realize that other people were able to see my worth and potential before I did. I guess that's why it was no question of having me stay. I HAD to leave in order for her to get control back of the classroom and be "in charge".

Well, time to regroup again. I tried getting Corey off my mind by giving him the silent treatment. I figured, "out of sight, out of mind." I needed someone else to divert my attention somehow. Chondra had introduced me to a guy she worked with named Jon Tisdale.

He was the most beautiful man I had ever seen up to this point. His body was chiseled to perfection, and he had a heart of sheer gratitude. He was in the process of marrying his girlfriend, who was expecting at the time. We began talking every day as friends. He was so charming and thoughtful. We were both Gemini, and whenever we saw our birthday come up on the clock, we would tell each other, "Happy Birthday." I loved conversing with him. Our chats were always meaningful to me. One day we had an opportunity to go out. Chondra had invited him and another guy from her job to hang out. We went to the bowling alley, then back to her house.

I had begun living with her once the job ended. Jon and I talked for a while and then went upstairs to be alone. He and I joined together in unison and became one that night. I had never felt so loved, protected, and admired as I did with him. He looked at me as if every scar and every flaw were like an enhancing mark of beauty. I honestly fell in love that night, or rather, I fell in love with the "image" of love. It hurt my heart when we had to end. He had a chosen path to be a father and family man. Although their parents forced them to marry for religious reasons, I had to honor, and respect his wishes.

Within a couple more months, Corey and I were pretty much done. Now he began dating this older woman. That really hurt me in a lot of ways. I felt like I was becoming a stalker, trying to figure out, "what does she have that I don't?" It was all a big mess for me. I literally had a dream that she was in his life. The dream was centered around a church event. I went to sit beside him, and he said, "No, this seat is taken." Within the dream, I saw this young lady come towards me to go sit in the seat. I couldn't distinguish her face, but I knew in my heart I had been replaced before I knew I was replaced. Since Corey was now gone, I had put Lenny on the back burner long enough. So, I decided to give him a call.

We both decided to meet up one night, and he used his cousin's car to pick me up. We didn't go far because I didn't have a key to get back into Granny's, so we ended up parking around the corner close to a dark alley. We both had the same intentions, and we got into the back of the car.

We looked at one another as if the long wait of anticipation had taken over us. As he kissed my neck, he prepared himself to enter my love box. I remember him pumping and gyrating on top of me, but honestly, I didn't feel anything. When he was done, he was huffing and puffing as if he had just run a sprint. He climbed off me and I looked down at his package. Needless to say, it lacked any girth, width, or power for that matter. This nigga had a baby foot for a dick! Go figure. All this time, I had waited to be with this guy, and all I could say to myself was, *"Damn, this won't shit."*

Chondra and I had devised a plan to get our lives together. She was going into the army like her older brother and convinced me that we should do the buddy system. So, I took my ASVAB test for entry into The United States Army and passed with flying colors. The only thing left was to pass the physical, and according to the recruiter, I was NOT physically fit. I weighed in at 155 lbs., thanks to Mrs. Quinn and us walking every day. The recruiter at the time suggested that I lose another 10-15 lbs. to complete my entry, and she would help me to do it.

I put into my mind that I was going to do this and live a totally different life away from it all. Chondra decided to have a going away party since she had already been given her departure date for basic training. Being that I still lived with her, I would be the chef for the party. She had plenty of liquor and snacks and had set up a DJ to come to this house party. So, we all took part in partying before the official party started. A few of her high school friends named Tisha, Angie, Bradley, and a girl named Andi came too. We all were getting "lit." We had enough smoke and drinks to last for hours. As time passed, we noticed that no one else had arrived. I mean, this is the country, and word travels fast when a party's happening. Chondra decided to investigate why no one was there. She was determined to find out where the people were and to bring them to her house. Little did we know, there was another party going on at the SAME time. So, we all got in her Hyundai to drive over there.

Omg, I was torn up. I knew I was inebriated from the drinking, but I didn't realize how much the drinking and the smoking had taken a toll on me until I got in the car. My head felt so heavy as she would turn on the winding roads. I felt like a bobble head the way it uncontrollably went from side to side. When we finally made it to the other house, there were so many people. It looked like the whole county was in this one backyard. They had these huge speakers on each side of the house, and the bass was so loud from the music that it made the ground tremble. As we walked around, she walked up to people, yelling over the music to have them come to her party instead. I felt like I was at the Homecoming concert at VSU all over again. My vision was so blurred that I couldn't see a thing if you weren't in front of me. Walking through the crowd, I was able to spot Bradley, who rode with us.

"Hey Bradley, I need you. I can't see shit. Can I hold onto you to walk me through the crowd?"

"Girl, come on. You fucked up for real." he said. I just laughed in response as I clutched onto his arm while he guided me back to the car. Although Chondra's efforts were thwarted, we all went back to the house and continued the party by ourselves.

Back at the house, we were all laughing, joking around, and eating the food I'd prepared earlier. Like Granny, I made fried chicken well. So, Chondra wanted me to make it for just about every gathering that she had. It was getting late, and we were all getting a bit tired, so Chondra told everyone to stay the night so they wouldn't drive drunk. Two of the girls had already gone upstairs to bed. Bradley looked at me and asked, "Can I come up with you?"

'Sure, ok," I said. Both of us were extremely intoxicated, and whatever attraction we had was solely based on that. He wasn't my type, and I was definitely not his. But that night, the interaction between us was exciting and earth-shaking. Not in a lovemaking way, but in a down-and-dirty kinda way.

Chondra happened to come into the room mid-way, and we kept on going as if she wasn't there. That's how intense it was. The next morning, we both looked at each other, and he said, "Can we do that again?" Nevertheless, I gave him the nod of approval.

Over the next few weeks, I mentally prepared myself for working out with the recruiter. I had to do a military diet and shed those few pounds so that I could get a departure date. Something wasn't right, and I began feeling kinda funny. Chondra would smoke all the time and it never bothered me until now. The smell of the smoke turned my stomach. Then I began craving shrimp fried rice and strawberries. I just thought it was weird and didn't think too much of it. This didn't seem new to me. I had weird cravings anyway during my menstrual period. For a while, I could only drink Lipton Brisk tea with Lemon two weeks before my cycle.

That was the only thing that quenched my thirst. Chondra, some of the girls and I decided to go to the county fair. When we got there, there were bright lights everywhere. But my stomach was doing somersaults from all the different aromas in the air. "What in the world is going on?" I thought to myself. I couldn't put my finger on it. Then I noticed how baby commercials caught my eye every time I watched television. The first thought that came to mind was, "Am I pregnant? I can't be. Am I though?" Questions began to loom through my mind constantly. One night while at Chondra's, I was sleeping upstairs in one room, and Angie was in the other room with a guy. Chondra was downstairs on the sofa, with another guy sleeping in another room as well. I was awakened by a scratching noise against the wall. It was dark in the room, so I thought it was one of those beetle-looking bugs that buzzed around the walls. The sound was becoming irritating, so I turned on the light. To my surprise, it was a bat. It was hanging upside down, flapping its wings against the wall. I was in shock. I had never seen a bat up close, and I was contemplating a way to get out of the room.

I finally made a way of escape downstairs and was trying to tell Chondra what had happened. She was half asleep herself, and my story became bothersome to her rest.

"Girl. Oh my God. Oh my God. You wouldn't believe what I saw upstairs." I said while my body was trembling.

"Damn, Shawaun, I'm tired. Tell me in the morning." she said. Suddenly, another bat came flying into the room where we were, then flew back into the kitchen. I was trying to get her attention again. She was getting really irritated by me at this point, but I was trying to show her the bat that flew in here.

"Chondra, there it is again, WAKE UP." She woke with extreme irritation and damn near fell off the sofa when she saw the unexpected visitor. "AAAAAHHHHH." We both screamed. She looked at me with complete terror in her eyes. We were both scared. The screaming woke up everyone upstairs. Angie and the two guys came down looking puzzled.

"It's a freaking bat flying around in here." Chondra said to them.

"No it's two of them. One was in my room. That's why I came down here." They all looked at me with the same expression, "What the hell?" One guy ended up getting the one out of my room, and that one came flying downstairs as well. After a bit of a struggle, the guys were able to get both bats out of the house. I felt so relieved, as I'm sure the other girls were as well. Even though the bat was out of the room, I couldn't go back in there just yet. I stayed downstairs on the sofa and slept until later in the morning. After the sun had risen, everyone began coming downstairs. The two guys decided to leave, and the girls and I began to sit around and talk. The weirdest thing about their conversations was that they each dreamed of death or someone who already died.

Chondra dreamed that we were going to her Momma's funeral. She called her grandmother "Momma" since she raised her, but she was very much alive and lived down the road. Then Angie said her dream was about her grandfather, who had died a few years back. In my mind, that was ALL the confirmation I needed. I was pregnant. Here I was, surrounded by people dreaming about death. My Granny used to say that death meant there was life coming. And I KNEW I had life growing inside of me. I had a test done which confirmed that I was indeed pregnant. Any desire to go into the Army now was out of the question. I wasn't going to have my baby raised by someone else.

The pregnancy was going well but I began having some heavy concerns. I really wasn't sure who the father of my child was. I kept a journal of everyone that I was with, my menstrual cycle, and everything in between. Unfortunately, I was quite reckless during that time. I was with Lenny one week, and Bradley the next. It could've been either one of them at this point! This is gonna be the longest 9 months ever! My siblings were watching my stomach grow over the course of my pregnancy with anticipation. Ayana was ALWAYS around me talking to my stomach. My little brother Darron was just watching how my belly was growing. While my other sister Shaunda, began having a really hard time. She became more distant and defiant at home. Granny had a different work schedule now that she was working at the hospital. Shaunda and I shared a bedroom together, so it was like the more stuff I would buy for the baby, the more resentful she became.

One night, Granny had left for her usual game of Bingo and left the older people in charge; meaning my Uncles' and I. Now my Uncles' only looked out if the kids were downstairs, so when they were upstairs, it was on me. I can't remember what the initial reason was that started the argument in the first place, but I think she had gone into something of mine without asking.

We ended up getting into a screaming match, which wasn't uncommon in our house. She grabbed something and threw it at me. I went over to her bed to spank her for doing it. As I got close to her, she leaned back and kicked me in my stomach and said, "I hope your baby dies."

It was as if she turned on the crazy switch for real. Before I knew it, I lunged for her neck to try and kill her. HOW DARE she wish death on my unborn child. At that point, I didn't care if she was my sister or NOT. She did not deserve to breathe the same air as me after that comment. I had literally pinned her down and was crushing her, almost suffocating her. Ayana tried to get me off her but couldn't. Then Baby Joe came upstairs from hearing all the commotion, and he and my sister were taking turns trying to get me off. They eventually broke us free, but from that point on, THAT little girl was enemy number 1.

When Granny got home that night, she had the nerve to say that I was wrong. "That's your sister Shawaun. You shouldn't treat her that way." I couldn't believe that she condoned that behavior at all. I don't give a fuck WHO you are. My baby is innocent in all this and should never be disregarded in such a way. That thing got in my spirit so deeply. Like, I couldn't bounce back from that at all. I began to distance myself from her. She was 10 years old at the time, and we were like 11 years apart. I had been like the mother figure to her since my Mom had been injured. She was 3 years old at the time of the accident, and God was telling me that I needed to talk to her. I was so damn mad though. I definitely had to cool off before I did.

A few days later I asked her, "Why did you feel like what you said about my baby was ok? Why would you hope my baby dies? Tell me?" And the words that came out of her mouth softened my heart a bit.

"When you have your baby, you're not gonna think about me anymore." All this time, I never thought about how this would affect my siblings.

"Shaunda, it's not going to change how I feel about you. It's just that now, I will have my own daughter to look out for. The things that I do for you and with you are because I WANT to do those things. It's not because I HAVE to. I'm NOT your Mom. I'm your sister. And what I do is because I choose to do them. I'm not obligated to do anything for you." I had to get her to understand that, but it went on deaf ears. That day changed the dynamics of our relationship completely. To this day, we still haven't recovered.

At the time, I was working as a receptionist at a sign company where I got to talking with one of my coworkers who happened to be of Vietnamese descent. His name was Tai. I fell in love with the name and wanted to know what it meant. He said the name meant "The Most High." That was it. I had to combine it in some kind of way for my daughter's name. I wanted her to have my initials, so I was going to name her Shai Tenae Jones. It wasn't the same, but she would now be my first priority. In my eyes, she was "the highest". As the time got closer, I was able to get her a beautiful white crib and a lot of baby stuff for her arrival. She was set to be born on March 17th, but she wanted to make her debut when SHE felt like it. The doctors decided to schedule an induction for the following week since she was taking her time.

They scheduled me for Wednesday morning at 8 am. That Tuesday night, I went out with some friends bowling. I started feeling funny that night, and I was having Braxton hicks contractions. I remember the whole night I was thinking about Corey and how much I missed him. My girlfriend ended the night early and took me home. On the way home, a song called "All My Life" by KC & JoJo came on, and I began to vent about how I felt about Corey. At the time, I knew my girlfriend was looking at me like I was crazy. But my heart was aching from what I felt was "my first forever love." I got home around midnight, but I really couldn't sleep. I tossed and turned most of the night while my belly was hardening every so often. By 4 am, I couldn't take the discomfort any longer. I went into Granny's room and told her, "Granny, I think I need to go to the hospital. I keep feeling like I have to shit, and nothing is coming out."

She looked at me and said, "It's time. Let's get ready to go." My sister Ayana wanted to tag along, so we all loaded up the car heading to the hospital. They got me situated in the room, and my little sister was sitting beside my Granny on the other side of the room. Granny had already given me tips of advice.

She said, "Don't be doing a bunch of hollering. It's not gonna change anything and will only make the pain worse. When you feel like you have to push, PUSH with all your might." So, I did just what she said, and at 6:25 a.m. on March 25th, Shai Tenae arrived.

I couldn't imagine myself being a mother. I was only 21 years old. I was the same age as my Mom was when she had me. Shai was the most adorable little being that I had ever seen. I couldn't keep my eyes off her. I refused to let the doctors take her to the baby room without me. The staff allowed her to stay in the room with me. When they took her out for testing, I would be right there with them to watch. I heard too many stories of people stealing babies that I didn't want that to be my fate. I needed to walk around anyway, and this eased my mind a bit. In my mind, this was a glorious moment in my life. All I ever wanted was to be happy anyway.

CHAPTER 10

NO MORE DRAMA

Shai has been growing by leaps and bounds. She is so smart. I think it's due to my breastfeeding. I decided that I wanted to give her the best start in life, and formula just wasn't it for me. My sister Ayana would come in every night before she went to sleep and would sing the Barney song to her. That was so cute. "I love you, you love me. We're a happy family. With a great big hug and a kiss from me to you (kiss sound). Won't you say you love me too." She sang this every night without fail. She was always around Shai, and I guess you could say she was like her little baby as well. At the time, she was 14 years old, so watching me gave her a view of the responsibility involved in raising a child; so that she would wait to have one of her own.

After her first year, we decided to move into our own place. It was not the best, but it was ours. We lived in Jackson Ward Projects, right at 1422 St. James St. I was excited to have my own place. It really took some getting used to because I had never lived on my own. I had reached out to Lenny before I moved, so he could see the baby. He came by and looked at her, but he denied her, which really hurt my feelings. But life goes on, right? I informed him that I would be sending his name to the child support enforcement office so that we could get a paternity test done. Shai was like the smallest thing around walking at church. She started walking when she was 6 months old.

It's so funny, she had been crawling around super-fast at Granny's house, and one day I had some ice cream. She was standing up by the chair beside Granny and was about 2 feet away from me.

I said, "Come on, Shai, stand up and walk over." She took the first two steps, and I didn't want to get excited because it would startle her, and she may fall, so I coaxed her over. In my mind, I was thinking, "YES, BABY GIRL.... YOU'RE DOING IT." But I had to remain calm until she walked over. Then I could cheer outwardly. She took the last few steps and then fell when she got close to me. We all cheered her on and were smiling and laughing at the same time. She did it, but we were laughing at how the ice cream was the REAL motivation for it all.

I had one of the deaconesses come up to me at the church, admiring how Shai looked and how fast she was growing. She said, "Shawaun, the Spirit told me that you're gonna have another baby within the next 3 years. Shai is moving out of the way for another one." I looked at her in disbelief. "Why is she putting ANOTHER baby on me?" I thought. But I guess we'll just have to see if the "Spirit" was right on this one. I ended up having a really bad experience with this guy I had met through the local gospel station, which held me back from wanting to date anyone. He was a disc jockey and was much older than me. Shai was six months old at the time, and he invited me over to his house. I allowed him to take advantage of me and performed oral sex. It wasn't that I hadn't tried it before with Corey, but this time, it was much more erotic, and a bit dehumanizing. It was my first time ever referring to a penis as a "dick." I know I referenced it earlier, but I had never SPOKEN it aloud. I thought that term was nasty and vulgar.

He kept saying how I had a "pussy", and he had a "dick", and that I needed to grow up and learn to love it. When he ejaculated in my mouth, it tasted disgusting, and I immediately ran to the bathroom to spit it out. I truly felt dirty afterward, to say the least. "How in the hell did I get myself into THIS situation?" On top of that, I had no transportation or money to leave and had no idea where I was exactly.

I had NEVER been in a position like this before and truly didn't know what to do or who to call. He left me and my baby in his apartment all day. I went into panic mode. I didn't eat anything out of fear, and only drank water. I had to at least keep some fluids in me to continue producing milk, since I was still breastfeeding. When he returned, it was around 5 pm in the evening.

"You're still here?" he said.

"Yeah, I didn't have a way to get home." He threw $40 cash on the bed, told me to call a cab, and walked out of the room; leaving for an event he had to emcee. I felt so cheap. I ended up calling a girlfriend I went to high school with that lived on that side of town. I had to describe to her where I was. Tina came and picked us up, and I cried in her car. Never had I felt so shameful as I did that day. I vowed to NEVER put myself in that position again. Yet as the saying goes, "Never say never." I had to learn this the hard way.

The summer was approaching, and I got a job with the church's children's camp. I was super excited because it reminded me of when I worked at the elementary school. With Shai being around two years old now, I decided to get back out there into the dating scene. I started off with a dating site since I didn't really get out much without transportation. I talked to a few guys over the phone before setting up a date with a guy named Jerrell. We went out bowling at first and had a good time. We talked more and then he invited me over to his home. We were young, and he lived with his parents still, yet very self-sufficient and hard working. He was not someone I would've chosen at all in the looks department, and he was a bit short. We were the same height, and I didn't favor short men at all, but he was really nice and gentleman-like, so it worked for me. When I went over, I had Shai stay at Granny's house, and Ayana watched her for me. We went out to dinner, and then we went back to his house. I wasn't attracted to him, but my loins were on high alert. I decided to indulge physically with this man, and to my surprise, it was GREAT.

I truly underestimated him. We talked just about every day. After our next date, he came to my apartment and we were intimate there as well. I became wrapped up in Jerrell for a minute, that I forgot all about my open profile on the site. I didn't close it, so I was still getting responses. I got a response from another man on there who was beautiful to me. He was 6'3 and had the most beautiful hazel eyes. I found out later they were contacts, but he was still cute to me. And with that, I brushed off Jerrell to get to know this other guy. He had the oddest name. His name was Theiascence. He had such a strong masculine voice and loved poetry and music like me. I noticed I've always attracted men with similar qualities, which made it easier for me to connect. He asked me out on a date after a few conversations, and we decided to go to Olive Garden. He picked me up from Granny's house because I didn't want him to know where I lived and didn't want to be JUDGED because of where I lived. He picked me up in an aqua-colored Honda Accord with silver rims with a hatch on the back.

I LOVED that model... It was the box-shaped kind which was like a classic to me at the time. I believe it was the 1991 model, and I wanted one just like it. We talked about it over dinner, and he said that he would give me the info from where he got his from. I was excited by that. He talked about his family, his 4-year-old daughter, and that he had a home in Chesterfield. He said his Mom and Dad were going through a rough patch, so his Mom had moved in temporarily, but that she was gone most of the time working, playing with her weekly bridge group, or with his Dad. He seemed like a pretty wholesome guy. I would soon learn that everything that looks good *ain't* good for you.

We began spending a lot more time together. He would pick up Shai and me from the church when I got off, and we would go back to his house. We were there almost 3 or 4 days out of the week. The house was not that clean, but I couldn't judge because my house wasn't the cleanest either.

They had a cat though which had urinated in spots all over the house. Then the cat had fleas, so Shai and I would get bit all the time. One day when he came to pick us up as usual, he came inside the church. The camp director was named Mrs. Gracie. She attended church, and we shared the same birthday.

She would always tell me her story of how she was a single mom of 3 girls for a long time before God sent her to her husband. She was very direct and old school but would do ANYTHING to help you out if you were struggling. She was such an awesome lady. There were times when I didn't have food, and she would have me come to her house and get whatever I wanted out of her freezer. She became like a second Mom to me. She gave me guidance, while imparting her wisdom which I truly needed. This particular day though, Theiascence was in a bad mood and was waiting for Shai to hurry up. When she came, he grabbed her by the arm and took her up the stairs.

The next day when I came in, Mrs. Gracie pulled me into one of the empty offices. She said, "Shawaun, I need to talk to you. Now it's really none of my business what YOU do, but when I see where one of my babies may be affected, I HAVE to say something." I looked at her intently and with great concern as she continued speaking. "The guy that picks you up every day, is he your boyfriend?"

"Yes, ma'am," I said.

"Well, yesterday, I saw him grab Shai in a way I did not like and pull her up the stairs to the car. Again, it's none of my business, but does he do this often?" Honestly, I didn't really see what had happened because I was distracted doing something else at the time. I sat there for a moment, trying to process this. I noticed at times how he was somewhat hard on her, especially with toilet training, but I didn't really think anything of it. He never disciplined her and left that to me. Hearing what she was saying took me aback a bit, but I was taught to respect my elders no matter what.

"Mrs. Gracie, I will definitely keep my eyes open from now on. Thank you for letting me know," I said.

Soon after, he noticed the relationship I was having with Mrs. Gracie and began to discourage me from spending time with her. He then suggested that I move in with him permanently. With hopes of finally being with someone that I felt truly loved me, I gave up my place and moved in. It's true when they say that you become "Dicmitized" and totally blind to the reality around you. I was really blinded by this one. Our first time being intimate together was the most sincere, loving experience I had EVER had up to this point. He not only took his time, but he watched me with every stroke as he memorized what made me feel the best. I LOVED that about him. And saw that he had great potential. He was really smart and self-taught in a lot of ways. He read books that I had never heard of and had studied psychology. He was like 4 or 5 years older than me, but in my eyes, I was learning from him; and valued whatever he said.

I moved in and soon left the job at the church since he said that was too far for me to drive every day. I ended up taking on another job at the newly opened Walmart down the street. I had found someone to watch Shai for me that was very reasonable, so I felt good about that. He would drop me off and pick me up every day. In the beginning, I thought this was great, but I soon realized the motive behind it. I worked there for a while helping to build up the store for its grand opening. By the time the store was open for a few weeks, I had ended up leaving there as well. He saw me talking to one of the guys at the job and became outraged by our interactions. Every day when he would pick me up, one of my co-workers named Shawn would walk me out. He was a real cool guy. Never once had he ever advanced himself on me. We had a brother-and-sister relationship, and he talked about his girl ALL the damn time.

They ended up getting married later as well, but at the time, they were just dating. Theiascence swore up and down we had a relationship or that we were intimate at work. To end the debate of all the drama brewing, I decided to leave the job altogether. We both would go to his friend's house in Varina since he was a member of the church that he and I were going to.

The church was in Varina as well, and it was a very small church, but the people were really nice. I noticed that the relationship between us was changing and that he was becoming very controlling. I felt like I was going out of my way to please him, but it was never enough.

When I would do little things with Shai, it was like he had a problem with it and wanted all my time to be showered on him. I was really going into passive mode and didn't say much to challenge him. On the home front, his story was beginning to unravel. The so-called house wasn't his at all. It was his mother's. And the "Dad" he was talking about didn't exist. He had never met or even knew who his father was. Then I found out that he was abused as a child sexually by someone his mother left him with while she went to work. I don't think he ever got over that and held that against her. He had a younger brother who would come to visit from time to time, and he would always ask me, "What do you see in my brother? You seem smarter than that." I never understood what he meant, but as I got deeper in the mess, it all made sense. His mother and I became close since we all LIVED together. She worked for the postal service and had been there for years. She told me a lot about their family in New York and how they were of Native American descent, and that her father was an entrepreneur with multiple businesses.

I found it quite fascinating to know more about their lineage. I asked her though why Theiascence acted the way he did towards her sometimes. And she said that she felt guilty for what happened to him and had been trying for years to make it up to him while putting herself in debt doing it. She told me that she took out the loan to get him the car I loved, and paid cash for it. As I was hearing all of this, I was in shock. "Who the hell did I meet? He lied about his WHOLE life. Mrs. Gracie was right. I should've paid attention." All I could think was how I was in too deep, and I didn't know how to get out of this.

The church we attended needed someone to work in their summer program and being that I had done this at my old church, this was pretty familiar to me. Theiascence "allowed" me to take the job, and by this time, he was no longer working at Coca Cola. All the lavish dining had ended, and things were a struggle. He even let me take the car and drive myself to work, which I thought was great. It gave me time to really try to clear my mind and have some time with God. At the church, the Pastor and his wife had fallen in love with me. Anything that I needed, they provided. I didn't like to ask them for much, or anything really, but they always offered. They would watch me interact with the kids and saw that my spirit was humble and loving. I remember one day he and I were getting ready for church. I had lost a lot of weight due to the stress of the relationship, and I asked Granny if she had something I could wear for this event they were having at church. She had a black dress in her closet from back in the day, that I asked if I could wear. She said "Sure, I can't wear it anymore."

The dress was form fitted and exposed the cleavage area. Being that I was heavily busted, I found a way to pin the top to not expose so much. I remember walking down the stairs of the house feeling like a million bucks. When I got to the bottom of the stairs, he said, "Why are you showing all of your titties? That's not appropriate at all. What are you trying to do? Snag the Pastor now?" The comment made me feel so low. I wasn't trying to tease anyone. I wanted to look good on his arm, but I guess he was repulsed by my efforts. That whole day during the service, I felt so self-conscious and was finding ways to keep myself hidden throughout the service. At work the next day, I was feeling kind of funny, but I didn't pay too much attention. I was feeling a bit light-headed, and the Pastor's wife had me sit down in her office. We talked for a while with general conversation, and then she asked, "Are you feeling ok, really?"

"Yes, ma'am," I said.

"Ok, my spirit is telling me it may be something else going on. Please go to a doctor so you can get checked out". Again, I'm not one to disrespect my elders, especially after the situation with Mrs. Gracie. I nodded in reply and walked out of her office. The thought had replayed in my mind all day. When I got back to the house, I was watching TV, and all of the baby commercials were catching my eye. "Oh shit, NO. I can't be pregnant again." I waited a few days to see if I was tripping, but the same feeling stuck with me, so I went and got a pregnancy test. To my dismay, it was positive. What the hell am I gonna do with another baby?

All I could think about was how I was gonna get away from this man. I HAD to at this point. We weren't really talking anymore, it was as if he irritated me so badly that I didn't want to be around him, and he noticed it by the way he treated me. One day, he decided to take me on a road trip to Charlotte. It seemed like forever getting there. But when we got there, I LOVED it. We went to the basketball stadium and took pictures outside, and then we went to the mall for lunch. He showed me this huge church and said that's where he wanted us to get married. It was beautiful. It was all pink and looked like a mansion times 5.

I began to think of why I grew to love him in the first place, and this was one of the reasons. He was so good to me that day that it almost made me forget about all the bad times. On the way back, it was turning dark. I remember he stopped at all the Coca Cola vending machines and stole the change from them. He still had the master keys from when he worked there and never returned them. I couldn't believe he had done it. Let alone have me with him. I was scared to tell anyone, so I told his Mom. She was always so nonchalant when it came to things that he was doing. Like how his brother kept coming over because he was getting all these hits to his credit report and didn't know why. He suspected that it was his older brother but couldn't prove it. Then he realized that he had a book of checks missing, but no one could ever find them. One day while finally cleaning the kitchen, it was disgusting by the way, his mother found the check book on top of the cabinet.

All this time, Theiascence had been bouncing checks on his brother's account. Once again, his mother covered him and offered to pay all of the debt off for him. It was like she was taking sides or trying to be the peacemaker between both of her children. I then noticed that my private area was developing a really bad odor, and I didn't know why. I went to the doctor, and they told me I had trichomoniasis, a sexually transmitted disease that causes yeast infections. In my mind, he was the only one I would've gotten this from because I wasn't with ANYONE else at all. I noticed that he would always say that he was going to work with his friend Smithfield from the church. Smithfield had his own business, but I didn't know what that was. One morning, I awaken earlier than usual. I decided to look through the so-called work bag that he took with him every day. In it, I found wiring, tools, and some condoms and lube. When I asked him about it, this fool had the nerve to say that these were items needed for the job wiring different buildings. BULLSHIT. I knew then I HAD to get out of there. At work the next day, I asked to speak with the Pastor. I told him EVERYTHING! I felt like my back was against the wall, and I didn't know what to do. And he sat there and listened to me vent and get it all out.
He looked at me and then asked, "Are you finished?"

"Yes, Sir," I said.

"Let me just say that I'm sorry you've had to experience this. You remind me so much of my own daughter, and I would never want her to endure any of what you've had to experience. I will say this, a man like that needs some serious help that you aren't equipped to handle. Don't allow yourself to diminish your value with someone who obviously doesn't value himself."

I began to sit in his office and cry. What did I get myself into? And he walked over to me and said, "Honey, just pray. God is going to give you a sign and a way out if you want it." And from there, I did just that. Every day I prayed, asking God to get me out of this situation. "God, if you get me out of this, I will never put myself in something like this again."

The next week, he decided to go out with Smithfield real early, saying they had a job to do. This was my opportunity. I called my best friend since age 14, Christion, and told him to come pick me up. I packed up everything I could and was ready when he got there. Theiascence had run into a snag about a month ago and asked me to get the car plates in my name. Like a dummy, I did. But today, I wasn't leaving without those plates. I took both of the license plates off the car and packed them with my things. As soon as Christion arrived, I secured all my clothes in his trunk and Shai in her car seat. When I got in the car, I felt a huge relief take over my body. I felt like I could breathe again. Tears began to well up in my eyes, and Christion noticed. "I don't know what you went through, but I'm glad you're out of it now." Here I was again, going back to Granny's, pregnant. I didn't even tell her at first. I kept it a secret for as long as I could.

Ayana and I ended up getting a job together at the local grocery store called Ukrops. It was a family-owned business where a lot of young people got their start. I worked up front as a cashier since I already had customer service and cashiering experience. I loved working there, and so did my sister. She had a fixation on their fried chicken and ate it just about every day. I made a lot of friends there that I talked to daily. A few in particular were Billy from Produce, Mr. Marvin and Ms. Helena from the Meat Dept., and Ms. Francis, who worked up front as a cashier with me. Billy was close to my age and really cute. He was in college working towards his bachelor's in business administration.

He and I hit it off right away as friends, of course. Mr. Marvin was a Pastor, and Ms. Helena was very astute in the Word. They each gave me encouragement each day when I was feeling down. Eventually, I had to tell Granny I was pregnant.

I told Ayana first and begged her not to say anything yet. I had begun getting threatening phone calls from Theiascence about the plates I took off the car. I had regained my power and wasn't going to give them back.

I boldly stated, "If you need plates, you know where to get them and it's NOT from me. DMV gives them out every day. You can go and get your own." He was furious. He then called me all kinds of obscenities, but I didn't care. He wasn't going to drive around with my name attached to those plates.

The day I told Granny, I was nervous as hell. I didn't know what she would think of me. But I couldn't keep covering up with the big shirts. "Granny, I need to talk to you about something," I said. She looked at me as if she were waiting for me to continue.

"Well, I found out that I'm pregnant. I've known for a while, but I didn't want to tell you, and now I'm not really able to hide it."

She then looked at me and said, "I knew it already. I was just waiting for you to tell me." I felt a bit at ease after that, but I knew Granny, and even when she seems like she's on your side, she can easily switch up.

I had gotten really close to Billy. He would bring me home sometimes from work, and he became a fixture in my family. Everybody knew of him. He even came to visit my Mom with my family. I still think I have that picture to this day that we all took with my Mom. He became a really good friend to me. He made me laugh at times when I wanted to cry. I felt like I was going into a deep depression again. It was beginning to be a chore to get up and go to work. All the people I had been friendly with, I was slowly distancing myself from. Ms. Helena took notice. She would talk to me every day and pour life into me. One day she stopped me in the back and asked, "What are you planning to name your baby?"

"I'm planning to name her Parrish."
She looked at me in disbelief and said, "No, she needs a name representing the gift of the spirit…how about Joy or Charity?" I said no to both of those. The name didn't fit me.

Then it was as if a light bulb came on in her head. "I've GOT it. Name her Fiona, it means Faith. You need some faith in your life right now, and you're gonna need every bit of it to get you through." I thought about it, and one thing for sure was I NEEDED some faith because I felt like I was losing it.

"I'm gonna think about it, Ms. Helena." And the rest of the day at work, I pondered on that name. "Fiona, I think I like it." The thought of that name would be needed to help me deal with what was coming.

I had gone to the doctor for my next prenatal check-up and scheduled ultrasound. When performing the ultrasound, the doctor said they could see what looked like a black spot on her brain. This freaked the hell out of me. "What does that mean?" I said. "It can mean a lot of different things, Miss Jones. Right now, we must determine what it is. Oftentimes, it shows early signs of trauma to the brain, which develops into the down syndrome. I really don't want to project that prognosis without further investigation. I'm going to have you come back next week so that we can do this again. Please make sure you let the nurse set a date for next week on your way out." And then he walked out.

All I could think was that something was wrong with my baby. What if she does have down syndrome? Then what? Would I love her differently? Would I keep her? Did I do this to her because I've been stressed and emotional? All these thoughts were going through my mind. The thought of my child having any imperfections scared me. This news put me in a deeper depression. I went to work the next day, and Ms. Helena saw the expression on my face.

As soon as I went to the back to see her, I burst into tears. I gave her the news, and immediately she said, "Shawaun, what did you say you were naming this baby? Fiona, right? So where is your Faith? Whose report are you going to believe? This doctor or the Ultimate Doctor? God is the Ultimate Healer, Baby." And she stood right there and began to pray over me. My stomach leaped when she prayed for me, and I knew that my Fiona was listening.

I went back to the doctor the next week for the follow-up visit, and as they were doing the ultrasound, the black spot was gone. He couldn't find it. I was lying there thinking, "Praise God. Praise God. Thank you, Lord." As time moved on, I began showing a little, but not as much as I did with Shai. She really blew me up. Fiona was all in my stomach. Billy was growing more attached to me and asked if he could be the baby's Godfather. I was honored that he would even want to. I really respected him. For someone who was close to my age, he showed me that all men aren't bad. I had been through so much already, and his genuine friendship was bringing me back to life.

The day began as normal, and I was up trying to toggle with my baby belly. I went to the bathroom, but nothing came out. I laid back down for a while, it was around 8 am, and my stomach was beginning to hurt. Granny was getting ready to leave for work. She had to be there at 9 a.m., so if I needed to go to the hospital, she wouldn't be the one taking me this time. I was trying to hold off as long as I could, but I was sitting there thinking about who I could possibly call to take me to the hospital. I couldn't think of anyone. By 9 a.m., the contractions were stronger and more frequent. I buckled down and called Billy. "I'm on my way," he said excitedly. It was as if he was ready and waiting by the phone. Within minutes, he was pulling up in front of Granny's house. He opened the door for me to get in the car, and you could see the fear and concern on his face. You would've thought this was his baby being born. He was acting like a proud father. So sweet. As we were driving along, every bump in the road surged another contraction.

He saw the discomfort through his peripheral vision and immediately said, "I'm sorry." The whole way, I was thinking to myself, "Man, I wish he was this child's father. He is so awesome." He was speeding the whole way there. I could see the anxious look on his face as he was speeding on the highway. Once we pulled up, he got me out of the car and walked me in. We got to the room where I would be seen, and we were awaiting the nurse or doctor to come in.

When the nurse arrived, she looked at him and said, "Congratulations, Dad. Is this your first?"

Billy looked a bit out of place but still stood firm in his position, "No, ma'am, I'm just here as support," he said as he glanced at me.

"Well, Ms. Jones, please get undressed, and put on this gown so that we can prep you for delivery. Take whatever time you need, and when I return, we can get started," the nurse said. They both stepped out so that I could change clothes. I went into the bathroom to change, and the contractions were so strong I could barely stand. The urge to push was getting more intense by the minute. I managed to get my clothes off, but the feeling was getting stronger still. I heard Billy come back into the room, and I yelled out through the door, "Billy, I need a doctor ASAP." While he was going to find a doctor, I opened the door, and the Nurse came into the room. As soon as I took one next step, my water broke, and I grabbed it between my legs because I could feel the baby's head. She immediately told me to hop onto the bed, but I couldn't fully get situated. I was halfway off, and the baby was literally in my hands. The nurse looked at me in amazement that I basically had this baby with no one around.

The baby was lying on the bed by the time Billy walked back in. He was shocked. "Man, I missed it." he said. I low-key laughed, but I could sense a bit of disappointment. The nurse did too, so she asked him, "Would you like to be the first to hold her?" His eyes lit up like a Christmas tree. For someone who wasn't a father that day, you would've thought he was. He was beaming with so much pride holding Fiona. This moment felt so good, but it was short-lived.

Later that day, I was resting in my room, and Fiona was right beside me as I had done with Shai when she was born. The nurses came by to take Fiona out for a moment to have her weighed and to check her vitals. She was such a beautiful baby, almost like a china doll. She was pretty big too. She weighed 7 lbs. and ½ oz.

To my surprise, Granny came up to the hospital to see me. She asked where the baby was, and I told her she had just left. Granny looked at me nonchalantly and said, "Congratulations on the baby. I talked to the hospital administrator, and they are going to help you find somewhere to go." I looked at her for a moment, "She gotta be kidding me. I know she's gonna give me at least 6 weeks to get myself together. "Why does she always gotta act so hard?" I thought. She began to speak again, "The administrator will be coming to talk to you about finding somewhere else for you to live because you can't come to my house." Again, the words fell on deaf ears.

"Ok, Granny." And then she left. No other words were spoken. I was sitting there like, "She is so dramatic. Like damn, I'm not gonna stay at your house long…Geez." Moments later, a lady came into my room, "Ms. Jones?"

"Yes," I responded.

"My name is Abbey Stephens, I'm the Hospital Administrator here, and I had a talk with your grandmother today."

My eyes began to widen as the words were coming out of this lady's mouth. "OMG, Granny wasn't joking. I really don't have anywhere to go when I leave here tomorrow. What the fuck am I gonna do?" As the lady was talking, I felt like I was in a Charlie Brown cartoon. Everything at this point was muffled. "Do you have anyone that you can call or who you can stay with?" "No, ma'am, not at this time" "Well, we will check back up with you before your release tomorrow. I'm so sorry this is happening, but you'll have to find somewhere, or we will have to get the authorities involved. Do you understand Ms. Jones?" she said. I nodded in approval only because all words had escaped me. I sat there and just cried and cried, not knowing what was going to happen to me. Not only did I have one, but now I have TWO babies and nowhere to go. I thought of people I could call, but no one came to mind. I decided to reach out to a girl I went to school with.

I had known her since middle school, named Melissa Carlton. Melissa was always so sweet, and at this point, she was my only hope. I called her and told her my situation. She was shocked as well by the reaction of my grandmother, yet she showed me empathy as well. "Let me see what I can do, Shawaun, don't give up hope. I'm going to call you back shortly, ok?" "Ok, Mel." And with that, I waited. They brought Fiona back in, and I looked at this beautiful, innocent baby and wondered why she would have such a rough start in life. She didn't deserve this. "I'm the worst mother ever. How could I put us in this situation? I thought. A few hours later, Melissa called me back. "Shawaun, my Mom said that you can come to stay with her. She said she could not rest knowing you and the girls have nowhere to go. I'm going to pick you up tomorrow to get you settled in. What time are you being released?" And once again, I knew God answered prayers.

One minute I had nothing, and now I have an option I wouldn't have known existed. The next day, as soon as I knew my discharge time, Melissa was right at the hospital. I purchased the car seat at the hospital gift shop before leaving, and we headed to her car. I had to stop at Granny's house to get my clothes and pick up Shai. Shai was a bit uneasy, not knowing where we were going. In my mind, I would never forgive Granny for this. The day she came into that hospital room was the day she became my enemy for real. Just looking at her made me even more resentful of her. I wouldn't say that I hated her, but it was damn near close. After packing my things, we headed toward her Mom's place. She lived in the Highland Park area of Richmond. Prior to that time, I frequented the area but never lived in it. Highland Park was known for some of its notorious activities.

We had to walk up the back steps to get to the door. Melissa's sister was there, along with one of her brothers. Everyone marveled over Fiona. She was such a beautiful baby. All I could think was, "I'm so tired. I need to lay down." Melissa helped me carry my things into her Mother's room, where the girls and I would be sleeping.

I sat on the bed, feeling like a stranger in a strange land. As I began to settle in, her family was so accommodating. One of them came to the room to check up on the girls and me about every hour. I couldn't move. I think at that point, I had fallen into a deep hole of despair with no way of getting out. Over time, I think they noticed that I was experiencing postpartum depression as well. They just didn't know how to handle it. I literally cried every day for about two weeks. I would barely eat, I wouldn't get out of bed unless I needed to use the bathroom, and sometimes, I just soiled the bed so I wouldn't get up.

Her family was trying so hard to help, but it was as if I wasn't there. Even when looking at Fiona, as beautiful as she was, it was like looking at an alien that I didn't want to be near. I had a true case of postpartum depression, and I made living around me unbearable. By the third week, I could tell Melissa's family was ready for me to go, and the feeling was mutual. I called Ms. Helena and told her my situation. She offered to have me and the girls come to stay with her for a while. I was so ready to leave, and I'm sure they were happy to see me go as well.

Ms. Helena was a no-nonsense type of woman. She was very beautiful and exuded strength, tenacity, and reverence for God. She had two boys, and one still lived with her. He was so tall for his age. He was like 13 or 14 at the time, and he was already 6'1", I believe. She was tough on him, but for good reason. She wanted to make sure that he would grow into a respectful young man. I admire that about her. When we arrived, it was surely an adjustment for us all. She set her ground rules coming in the door. You either abide by it or leave as you came.

I had nowhere else to go, so I had to fall in line. Things were well for the most part, and over time, I enjoyed being there, but I still felt somewhat trapped. It wasn't my space. I still had to learn to conform to someone else's regime. Fiona was breastfed as well and did pretty well with it.

Unfortunately, she couldn't continue as long as Shai due to developing thrush. So around 3 ½ months, we stopped. During that time Ms. Helena and I grew tired of each other. She wanted her space back, and I wanted my own. She then suggested that I find a shelter to go to. We ended up finding a temporary shelter called Caritas and were set to leave by the end of the week. I remember the day she dropped me off. It was bittersweet, to say the least, but the fear of the unknown was on both of our faces. When I walked in, the lady at the desk took all of my information and asked for my ID. She then had me sit down in one of the waiting areas before going to our respective sites.

This shelter had a different location each week that you were transported to for lodging until you were able to get a place of your own. This was such a rough ordeal having to get the girls ready every day at 5 a.m., eat, and then be on the bus to go back to the office by 7 a.m. On top of that, we couldn't stay there. We had to find somewhere to go from 7 am until 3:30 p.m.; then return before the bus left again. We did this routine for about 3 weeks before we were able to get an apartment in Highland Park. It was a duplex home, and we had the downstairs apt. It was only 1 bedroom, but we made it work. The shelter helped to furnish the place for us with everything we needed. It wasn't the best, but it was ours...and we finally had something to call our own.

Shai had started preschool, and Fiona was growing so fast. She had the biggest natural curls I had ever seen. She always smiled, even when it seemed as if there was no reason to. She was bright and bubbly, but I noticed that certain milestones weren't being met the same way as Shai. I didn't want to compare the two because I knew that each child develops differently. Yet I couldn't shake that there was a bit of a delay. I was no longer working at Ukrop's since having Fiona and was on public assistance, trying to make ends meet. Billy was right by my side throughout all of this. Anytime I needed anything, he was right there. He began scheduling his life around mine. It was like we were in a relationship, but we weren't, and we respected each other's boundaries.

We planned to go on a bus trip to Atlantic City, and we had the best time. Everyone on the bus thought we were a couple, which still surprised us. We had not been intimate with each other at all. I think we held back because we valued our friendship and knew that would only complicate things between us. Soon we decided not to hold back anymore. I think after the trip, we realized that we really did care for one another on a deeper level. We had an intimate moment, and it was like being on a cloud of pure bliss. Our energies erupted and collided with the ecstasy we had been withholding from one another for so long. We learned how to communicate as friends, which made love-making easier, because we were now showing each other all that we wanted to say physically.

He was great. And we both enjoyed each other even more. He would come over to the apartment all the time. I would cook him dinner, and we would watch TV together. Oftentimes he would play with the girls, especially Fiona. He loved her as if she were his own. I loved seeing them all together. It was like a little blended family that I loved being around.

I was having some issues with the rent once the rent subsidy had ended. My landlord was such a pervert. He was an older man named Mr. Charles. He would come over and check on the place and then comment on how pretty I was. I would always thank him while trying not to be rude. Yet I could sense he was being way more forward than I wanted him to be. One night he came over unexpectedly and did his usual walk around, and before leaving, he grabbed me by my waist and kissed me on the lips. He said, "I know you've been having a hard time with the rent, so I can help you, and you can help me work off what you owe. I'm here to help." I couldn't BELIEVE the audacity. Damn, am I just looked at as a fuck toy for men? This was getting to be ridiculous. If I were really that type of chic, I would've jumped on the opportunity. But it wasn't me, not at all. In spite of trying to catch up financially, we ended up leaving there and were back in a shelter.

We then went to a different shelter, called ESI, Emergency Shelter, Inc in the downtown area. While I was there, I worked with the Social worker to find some employment opportunities. Because I told him that I was skilled in doing hair, and he saw my work on some of the other residents and decided to help me out. He knew a lady that owned a salon and was checking to see if he could get an apprenticeship opportunity for me. He even offered to get all of my supplies for me, which was so cool. I had never had anyone invest in my cosmetology endeavors. Granny always said that that wasn't a good field for me to go in. "It's too many salons around, and why would you want to be on your feet all day? Find something else to do besides that," she would say. One day I was coming from the shop so I could meet the kids being dropped off from the daycare. When I walked in, there was a new lady working at the desk. She looked at me kindly and said "Hello, my name is Tabitha. Are you one of the new interns upstairs?"

I said, "No, I don't work here."

"You're not one of the new people that works upstairs?"

"No, I'm a resident here."

"A resident?" she said. "You don't LOOK like you belong here."

Immediately, I took that as a sign from God as to why I was brought to this place. It was so people could really see homelessness from a different perspective. You don't have to look dirty, disheveled, or be a typical beggar on the street. You could be someone who had a closet full of nice clothes but lost their job yesterday and couldn't afford to stay in your home. Or you could have just fallen on hard times.

There's a myriad of reasons other than being destitute and degrading to oneself. I demonstrated that other perspective. I fit the mold of what "didn't" fit in the eyes of society according to the image of what homelessness looked like. I changed that lady's viewpoint for many years to come after that. So much so she would come to my room and borrow my clothes since she said that I always had nice things. This was too funny.

I connected with the lady that came to the shelter for weekly bible study. She would come to the shelter every Tuesday and worked around the corner in the local hat shop. Some days I would go over there, and she would buy me lunch, and I would try on hats. Or she would sing spirituals to me, and she could sing too. And when she prayed, oh my, she would pray your shoes off. You would feel the heavens come down directly in your lap and rest there. I loved being around Ms. Carol. She invited my kids and I to her church which was like Shereica's church, so I felt right at home. At New Deliverance Evangelistic Church (NDEC), I learned so much under Bishop Glenn. He was an awesome man of God. Due to space, we had to move back to the Caritas shelter so that we could get put on the waitlist for immediate housing. This time, I was familiar with the routine, so it wasn't as bad. There was an older man working there named Mr. Ben. He was a very handsome man to be up in age. He was physically fit and had the most beautiful curly hair. He would always look out for the girls and me without showing too much favoritism.

Once again, we were there for about 3 weeks and were offered a place in the Creighton Court public housing area. It was located on the East End side of town, which I had never lived in, so it was extremely new to me. Again, we were offered everything that we needed for furnishing, so I didn't have to worry too much. Mr. Ben even offered to move our stuff in for us, which was great because I was limited on funds. Like clockwork, he came with our things and moved everything single-handedly. He was great. I was so appreciative of his helping us get settled. Before leaving, he said his goodbyes, gave me a kiss, and said,

"Is it ok if I come back over when I get off tonight?" Now, I somewhat had a thing for older men, and this seemed like a good opportunity to be "taught some new things."

"Sure, you can come back."

"Ok, I'll be here around 10 tonight, that's ok?" he said, and I nodded in agreement. When he came over, I didn't expect my wig to get thrown off, yes literally. OMG, he did some things I've NEVER done sexually. He gave me a whole new respect for older men. Although looking back, it was so not right. I wasn't mature enough then to really understand the magnitude of the situation. Nor what the root stimuli was, but at that moment I was cool with it.

After further testing, it was discovered that Fiona had some developmental and speech delays. She is almost 3 years old now, and she just learned to walk at two, but she didn't have much vocabulary at all. She only said "Ma," and that's it. Because of this, she qualified for Supplemental Social Security, and they are going to pay retroactive from her birth. This was like the biggest breakthrough that I needed right now. God sure does answer prayers. Also, I got word from the Child Support office saying that they had gotten back in contact with Lenny and submitted the order for the paternity test. It's been a little over 4 years now, and I really wanted to get this over with. We finally had the appointment for the scheduled testing. I took Shai in with me, and they swabbed the both of us, and it was pretty easy. We were out of there in no time. Another month had passed, and I got the results in the mail.

I felt like I was on Maury, and how all the women on there say the same thing "I'm 100% sure he is the baby daddy." Only to find out they were wrong. Well, it was my turn, because the results determined he was NOT her father. That only left one other choice, Bradley. I reached out to Chondra since she was back in the states from her tour in Germany. I told her the situation and asked if she had Bradley's contact info so that I could inform him to get the test done.

"Are you sure you want to do this?" I didn't understand what she meant by that. "What do you mean? I want him to be aware that he has a child out here. What could possibly be wrong with that?" I said.

"Well, you know he is full-blown gay now. I just don't want to be involved with it all."

I'm sitting there listening to this bullshit like, "What the fuck is going on? She's not involved at all. It's not like I fucked HER and got pregnant." I couldn't believe that the girl I called my "friend" was denying me AND my daughter the right to inform this man that he was a father. Some kind of friend she is. This made me understand that some people in life will keep you in a box so that they can plateau ahead of you or feel like they do. I felt as long as I was struggling, she had an "upper hand". I may be wrong, but that was how I felt. And with that, I slowly backed away, but it wouldn't be long before we crossed paths again. I lived in the apartment for about 3 years in total. I went through a lot of changes and gained more maturity being here. I remember how one of my caseworkers with the CHIP program would come to my house for visits and would always say, "Wow, Shawaun. Outside it seems like a war zone, but as soon as I walk into your home, it's like I entered a peaceful place. You definitely haven't allowed this environment to become you."

Baby Joe was such a great help to me here. As I transitioned from job to job, he has been my babysitter through it all. I trust him with my kids, and as long as I have food, cable, and a box of cigarettes for him, he is here. I loved him for that… With the kids being in school, I took the opportunity to go and take the US Postal Service exam. It's rare that they host one locally, so I jumped at the opportunity. Being there was like being at a high school reunion. I saw so many people I hadn't seen in years. As I was walking to a seat, I saw one of my old classmates, Charles Daniels. He was looking real good after all these years. "Hey, Charles," I said as I was walking to the seat nearby. "Hey stranger, good to see you." he responded. The test was not that hard at all, and I felt pretty good about it. I was walking out, heading to the bus stop across the street, when my spirit said, "Go back and wait for him to come out." I walked back across the street to wait, and stood outside for a while to wait for Charles to come out.

While waiting, I ran into my old buddy, Shawn, from Walmart. We were catching up outside, and he was telling me that he had a daughter soon after I left. Come to find out, our daughters have the same first and middle names. That's crazy. We were standing there for a good minute when I saw Charles walking out. I didn't want to shake Shawn while he was talking abruptly, but in my mind, I wished he would hurry up. I politely interrupted him and told him I wanted to catch up with someone. I ran around the corner because I wasn't sure if he had left. I saw him get into his truck, and I walked by the vehicle and said, "Hey. I was trying to catch up with you. How have you been?" "I'm doing good. Did you need a ride?" he said. "Sure." I then hopped in the vehicle, not knowing where this would lead.

EPILOGUE

With life now taking so many unknown turns, it only makes me wonder how things will turn out. I finally feel like life is beginning to smile on me. So much of the bad is behind me, but is it really? Have I REALLY overcome? Or am I just waiting to run into the next brick wall around the corner? It's funny how life unfolds. Just when we think we've got it all together, here comes another blow. Time and time again, I've been **hit**, **punched**, even had the **wind knocked out of me**, yet I kept going. From the outside, I looked unscathed, but inside I was bleeding internally. It's only a matter of time before I began to **bleed on others**.

And the story continues…

THE LOTUS VISION

One day God was holding a bunch of seeds in His hands. He spoke over them different gifts, looks and talents that awaited them as they grew. He opened His hand and blew out breath of life, as each one flew out into the world.

All the seeds blew in different directions not knowing where they would land. Some landed on soil, some hit the ground. Some seeds were nurtured more than others, while some were left unfound. Many grew hardened to life elements, but still chose to survive. Then some never left the cracks where they fell, never to develop their purpose, or live to tell. But the seeds that descended into the water had bigger destines to fill! All because God had something special planned for them in His will!

It would not be an easy journey, and not many would pass the test. For He knew the ones that would hold onto His promises and prove to be the best. Only these seeds were brave at heart, prepared for the challenge - Ready to fight from the start. Hoping to fulfill the visions to come, while holding onto the promise of God, the Father, and Son!

They fought through the darkness although they were afraid. They stood firm during the storms and waves, held on through the rain. They cried many nights while they sat all alone. But God was watching and keeping them safe from harm. As each day passed, they grew a little more-a bit wiser than the days before! They dodged some of the weeds that were in the way. At times they became tangled but managed to break away. Weighed down by the elements surrounding them-still pushing through it all! Not knowing if they would find their purpose or fulfill His call. Yet their greatest feat was yet to be tackled. If conquered, their spirit would be free, or forever bound and shackled!

Many times, they had chosen to deviate from His path. No thought of the sins they'd commit, or pain from the wrath. But now, the pressure of their lives were too much to bear! They thought God had turned His back and no longer cared. "Where are you, Lord? How could you do this to us? This is not the life you promised when you blew us out like dust!" Then without notice, they heard a still small voice that interrupted their rage… wallowing in the pity of their emotional cage.

"If you would **TRUST** me and continue to **BELIEVE**…
I will pour out many blessings you haven't room enough to receive!
So don't be discouraged, or worried during this time…for it will not last.
Remember my seed, this too shall pass!"

With their bodies budding into form, they cried in sorrow and shame. Even when they felt defeated, God was STILL calling their name!!! And with their arms outstretched, they pushed toward their treasure. Holding onto the life changing message through each passing measure!

Looking back, we are like those seeds. Many are still at the bottom of the sea, too crippled to reach for the light. Not knowing whether to go to the left or to the right. Some of us are constantly floating, wondering where we will end up next. Never being able to take root, or to even find rest. Some of us coast through life living only for today. Looking for somewhere to go…searching for a place to stay. While the chosen few of us have been challenged to blossom to this VERY HOUR!!!!

This is why God created you…***Lotus Flower***
For even the most beautiful things can grow from the most troubled waters!
You are God's strong, beautiful and wonderfully made daughters'!